Testimoı

G000118060

'Sometimes in life we can appear to (on the outside while we know we are crumbling and crying out on the inside. It can be an extremely lonely and confronting place. *Conscious Grit* is the handbook to let you know you are not alone, and to help take you from stuck to unstuck. Gail's honest, heart-wrenching story connects as she holds your hand and helps guide you from feeling helpless to feeling empowered and in control. Whether in life or in business, *Conscious Grit* can help you manage yourself, your interactions with others, be a more effective leader and contributor and give you the toolkit you need to dance your way into building your ideal life, the way you want it.'

Nicole Nighthawk
Singer-Songwriter, Presenter, Photographer, Designer
Australian Independent Rock Artist of the Year, 2016

'In *Conscious Grit*, Gail Eaton-Briggs shares so much of her life and work experiences, that readers of her book will find numerous ways their own experiences overlap with hers. Since reading her manuscript I have told family and friends her book addresses the issues challenging some of them right now, like managing up and down, valuing sideways career moves and remaining resilient in the face of uncertainty. In addition to diagnostic tools and recommended strategies like finding a mentor or coach, Gail provides a gritty but accessible takeaway model for the reader that is based on both scientific evidence and her own rich experiences. A key aspect of her model is its emphasis on effectively working towards goals while accepting that life and careers are never linear.'

Dr John Mitchell, Consultant on staff skills and innovation in the education and health industries and the public sector

'I'll admit, books about personal development have never really appealed to me because they make me feel overwhelmed, like I need to change 100 things about myself or my practices right then and there! This book didn't make me feel pressured to do that. It made me see how much my 'crap-hands' have actually worked to make me the person I am and that person is actually okay. It has also made me see that being stuck in your ways is so detrimental to growth and that if you don't try you'll never know.'

Rebecca Hesman, Teacher

'Unlock your potential! Gail uses her own responses to a series of deeply personal challenges to help her move from stuck to becoming her own game changer. Treat this book as a guide to conscious problem solving. Use mapping tools and strategies provided by the author to help you set goals, plan and act. Gail will help you find the key to start reaching out, moving ahead and living life the way you want to.'

Stella Conroy, Not for Profit sector Executive committed to social justice, human relationships and the worth of individuals

'In all the professional and personal interactions that I have been privileged to have had with Gail over many years, I have found her tenacity, integrity and positive outlook to be some of her greatest strengths. Combine those with a fabulous personality and willingness to help others, and you have a woman who has all the necessary traits to be successful in any venture or task undertaken by her. Having read her book, a great deal of why Gail possesses these attributes were explained, and her suggestions for managing life and business are invaluable.'

Diane Tompson, Managing Director, The Powercom Group Commissioner for the Pacific and Asian regions for FCEM, (Les Femmes Chiefs d'Entreprise Mondial)

Conscious Grit

Conscious Grit

From stuck to unstoppable

Gail Eaton-Briggs

Published by Gail Eaton-Briggs

First published in 2021

Copyright © Gail Eaton-Briggs

www.everywhensolutions.com.au

The moral rights of the author have been asserted.

All rights reserved. Except as permitted under the Australian Copyright Act 1968 (for example, a fair dealing for the purposes of study, research, criticism or review). No part of this book may be reproduced, stored in a retrieval system communicated or transmitted in any form or by any means without prior written permission.

All inquiries should be made to the author.

Other than where explicit permission has been received, this book uses blended case examples to enforce the meaning behind the relevant chapter. Identifying information has been removed.

Every effort has been made to trace and seek permission for use of the original source of material used in this book. Where the attempt has been unsuccessful, the publisher would be pleased to hear from the author/publisher to rectify any omission.

Disclaimer

The material in this publication is of the nature of general comment only, and does not represent professional advice. It is not intended to provide specific guidance for particular circumstances and it should not be relied on as the basis for any decision to take action or not take action on any matter which it covers. Readers should obtain professional advice where appropriate, before making any such decision. To the maximum extent permitted by law, the author and publisher disclaim all responsibility and liability to any person, arising directly or indirectly from any person taking or not taking action based on the information in this publication.

Typeset by BookPOD

Front cover design by Olivia Duggan – Red Letterbox Design

ISBN: 978-0-6451157-0-3 (pbk)   ISBN: 978-0-6451157-1-0 (ebook)

 A catalogue record for this book is available from the National Library of Australia

Preface

When I was 22, my then husband and I experienced an event. It affected us, our children and families badly; we all suffered in individual ways. However, it wasn't until my daughter reached the same age that the intensity of what we'd been through, how I'd dealt with it and what I'd learned hit me.

I looked at my daughter: the smart, sassy, kind and thoughtful 22-year-old Alanna, and remembered myself at the same age and what my life had been like. I had a classic 'aha' moment. It was then that I thought, 'How the hell did I get through it? Where did the strength come from?' I had been just a kid when my world fell apart. I emerged from the ruins doing the best I could, but really, I was stuck.

In the past several months as I've transitioned from executive roles to establishing my own practice, Everywhen Solutions, I've reflected on how I got unstuck and achieved lots of things that have been meaningful to me and others. During this intense reflection, the concepts of conscious and unconscious grit came to me. These concepts are the core of my model for moving from stuck to unstoppable.

I'm telling my story now because, whilst the event and its ramifications were incredibly painful, the learnings that I've taken from it have been a gift that I will be grateful for, forever. I believe that we go through experiences for a reason and now I want to share mine with you to help you navigate this crazy thing we call life.

I've had challenges since – both personal and professional – and I know that my ability to move from stuck to unstoppable has served me well through the years.

If I could create a magic blanket and wrap it around you so that my experience and learnings would infuse into you, I would. Magic blankets aren't real though. So, I write in the hope this book will serve you well instead.

This book/blanket will warm you, strengthen you, inform you, energise you and help you. It will provide clarity and inspire you to make better choices and take decisive action. It will help you to overcome limiting beliefs that you may hold. You will be able to commit to becoming unstuck. Once unstuck, you will be unstoppable in pursuing your goals and aspirations.

Glossary

Catalyst moment – an event (negative or positive) that challenges or disrupts. Catalyst moments are golden learning moments.

Grit – the collection of personal traits that are characterised by bravery, spirit, courage, consistency, toughness, tenacity, strength, and passion. You may have heard people label others by saying 'he or she is really gritty'. In the context of this book, being gritty is a positive state – unless it's overdone.

The zone of conscious grit – the zone where an individual is persistent, determined, tenacious, resilient, acting with 'big C' Courage, has a future focus and makes plans.

Tipping point – the key to moving from the zone of unconscious grit to conscious grit.

The zone of unconscious grit – the zone where an individual is persistent, determined, tenacious, resilient, acting with 'little c' courage.

Unexpected crap-hand – a term I've invented to mean an event that happens where:

- there is no obvious fix
- there are life-changing adverse effects
- only you know how bad it is
- someone else is adversely affected
- all your choices affect others
- others won't be happy with your decision
- there are long-term impacts to physical and or mental health.

Unstoppable – whatever that term means for you. It will be different for each of us.

Contents

Preface   v

Introduction   1

PART ONE

Chapter One: The unexpected crap-hand   7

Chapter Two: It's a gritty world   25

Chapter Three: Find your tipping point into the
                zone of conscious grit   51

PART TWO

Chapter Four: Goals and planning   65

Chapter Five: Be ready. It won't be pretty   83

Chapter Six: You don't know what you don't know   101

Chapter Seven: The dance begins   135

PART THREE

Chapter Eight: The zone of conscious grit and the
                right brain   153

Chapter Nine: Live life 'like a boss'   183

Chapter Ten: Conscious grit can be overdone   219

Epilogue   243

Books and articles   247

Acknowledgements   249

Introduction

Sometimes I lie awake at night and ask, 'Where have I gone wrong?' And then a voice says to me 'This is going to take more than one night.'

— Charlie Brown, *Peanuts*

If you are having thoughts like Charlie Brown, this book will help you.

I use the story of being dealt an 'unexpected crap-hand' when I was 22 to show you how I was able to keep my kids safe and then create a good life. I became unstoppable.

We all have our own definition of what 'unstoppable' means. For me, once I started to get momentum through living in the zone of conscious grit, I found that opportunities opened up to me, and I had confidence to grab them and create more pathways to enrich my life. I have lots to share with you with the aim that you will be a step ahead of me. You'll know the traps and pitfalls. You'll have information that I didn't have at the time I needed it. You will see that it's possible to get unstuck and be unstoppable.

There are three parts to the story that I want to share with you.

Part One is my story and how it inspired me to create a model that others can use and benefit from. I'll tell you more about grit and how to get into the zone that will help you most – the zone of conscious grit. You'll find this in Chapters One to Three.

Part Two gives you all the information and knowledge that I now know but didn't know then. You'll find this in Chapters Four to Seven.

Part Three gives you many capabilities that you can add into your life in conscious grit. These are the skills and tools that I've learned over the years. I've chosen those that have been most impactful in all areas of my life. You can use them in the workplace, with your family, in good times, and when you need to fix up a mess. You'll find this in Chapters Eight to Ten.

'Grit' is a word that people have different opinions about.

When I think that someone's 'gritty' I see it as a good thing. My model, though, challenges the assumption that all grit is equally good; I say there is grit and there is even better grit.

There are some people who associate the trait of 'grit' with aggressive, achieve-at-all-costs, tread-on-other-people behaviour. This book is not about that type of grit.

I'm grateful for my grit. I have it in spades and have needed it repeatedly in my life through various personal and professional challenges. In talking to and observing others over the years, I've seen many examples of people with grit. I admire those people who have grit and use it wisely.

I have designed a model that helps individuals, who are already gritty, understand why they are stuck. I define this state as being in the 'zone of unconscious grit'.

In the zone of unconscious grit, you are trying hard by using your powers of persistence, determination, tenacity, 'little c' courage and resilience. There is no shame in being in this zone – but it's hard work and progress is limited.

There is another state of being: it's when you are living in the zone of conscious grit. Here, individuals combine tenacity, determination, persistence, 'big C' Courage and resilience with a focus on the future and a commitment to planning.

It's never too late to move into the zone of conscious grit. I was in the zone of unconscious grit for nearly five years. I was stuck.

Getting to the zone of conscious grit might be elusive. You need to find and catch a tipping point. It can be done, and I will tell you how I did it.

In this book you'll find models to guide you, words to motivate you, personal projects to do, information from researchers, and tips and tools that I've used.

By the end of the book, you'll be able to say with confidence, 'I don't deal the cards. I play the ones I'm given, and I do it really well.'

You will also say, 'I was stuck, now I'm unstoppable.'

PART ONE

CHAPTER ONE

The unexpected crap-hand

*One day you will tell the story of your life and
it will be someone else's survival guide.*

— Author unknown

The story — my unexpected crap-hand

In this chapter, I tell you about an event in my life. The event is one that I wish had never happened. Yet strangely, I know that experiencing all that I did pushed me to grow and develop confidence, capabilities and skills to have a life that maybe I wouldn't have had otherwise. I've taken those capabilities and skills into the workplace and had a good life and a good career.

Before the age of 22 years and 10 months, I had no idea that life could deal an unexpected crap-hand. Until 11 November 1981, I thought failed relationships, pets getting run over, and grandparents dying was as bad as life got. I knew people suffered — for example in car crashes — but that all happened to other people. I'd been well-conditioned as a child of the '60s and '70s: find a partner, work hard, play fair, get on with others, and all will be okay. Live within your means, and don't be a show-off. My well-meaning, loving and supportive parents role-modelled that and encouraged me, gently and not so gently, to follow that path. It was their path. It was the path of their parents. That's what they knew.

We all have a vision of how life will be. Mine was standard for the times. It included having a happy marriage that lasted until one of you died. I wanted a career in teaching, but I was discouraged from pursuing it. I was encouraged to get married.

Peter and I married before I turned 19. I was happy, working in an organisation that approved credit for people wanting to buy cars, furniture, and musical instruments. Baby Boomers like me remember those times before credit cards, when 'hire purchase' was used by most householders to furnish and equip their homes.

In the mid '70s, my dad decided to open a Retravision store, selling household electrical goods, with Mum, Peter, and me as business partners. We were excited. Both Dad and Peter left their jobs to begin the business. Dad had managed similar stores for years. It was an obvious next step for him. Peter was a natural salesman and could turn his hand to anything. It was going to be great.

The business grew. Within a couple of years, Mum left her role as a teacher's aide and joined them at the shop. The shop outgrew its premises and moved down the road. All was good in the world. At 22, I found out I was pregnant. We were all over the moon — including my two younger brothers, Peter's family and my beautiful grandmothers. The baby was due in November 1981.

In October, Peter, then 27 years old, developed severe headaches. He sought medical advice several times over a couple of weeks, including three times in one week when his headaches became so intense, he held his head in his hands and cried. The diagnosis was that they were due to tension, and there was no further testing.

The day my world changed forever, 11 November, started with excitement for me. I had a new recipe book, and the baby was only a couple of weeks away from being born. I decided to buy some ingredients and make a nice dinner.

I arrived home around 3 pm and found Mum's car out the front. Remember, this was pre—mobile phone days. I had no idea what was awaiting me. When I walked around the back of the house, Peter was lying semi-conscious under a tree, with my mum kneeling beside him, trying to keep him talking. We called an ambulance, and the emergency doctors put the then unconscious Peter into intensive care.

He had suffered a cerebral haemorrhage, which is a type of bleed that occurs within the brain. The doctors in the Intensive Care Unit of the hospital believed he would not wake up. Previous medical examinations hadn't identified his condition. They had missed the aneurysm, or swollen blood vessel, that led to Peter's haemorrhage. Once it had burst, it was too late to prevent the bleeding in his brain, and it caused significant damage. Over the next few days, Peter remained unconscious. The neurosurgeons looked for signs that he'd stabilised enough for them to operate and stop the bleeding.

Both Peter's doctor and my obstetrician agreed it was best to induce our baby before Peter's surgery. The outcome of his operation was in doubt. On 23 November, in between contractions and while holding my mum's hand, I signed consent for his surgery to be done the next day. And that was when Jason was born.

Peter survived, but they could not clip the aneurysm. They used a tendon to wrap it, hoping that this would stop the bleeding. After ten days, baby Jason and I moved into my parents' home. Dad held down the business on his own. Mum supported Dad, and she was also a rock for me.

Then six weeks later, while still in hospital and recovering from the first surgery, Peter had another bleed. The surgeon told me that Peter needed more surgery and that a positive outcome was unlikely. This time, the surgeons managed to get the clip in place and stop the bleeding. But more damage had been caused. It was several weeks before Peter came home from hospital to live with our baby and me in the front room at my mum and dad's home. Peter needed rehabilitation for speech, walking, memory, and coordination. But he was home, and we had a healthy baby. I was optimistic.

Reality set in. Peter drenched the bed with massive sweats each night. He now had severe epilepsy. His seizures were frequent, unpredictable, and scary. He showed little emotion. His brain injury affected many aspects of his physical, cognitive, and executive functions. He struggled with impulse control, emotional control, flexible thinking, working memory, self-monitoring, planning and prioritising, task initiation, organisation, decision-making, abstract reasoning, judgement, short-term memory, and sustaining attention. (I came to learn all the technical terms.)

His personality had changed too, but Peter didn't understand what he had been through and the damage caused to him. He was distant and apathetic. He was confused, and his behaviour was unpredictable. Our relationship was severely affected. Peter didn't understand safety and why I was so pedantic about safety around Jason. He thought I was being difficult. Trust was disrupted for both of us. I realised I couldn't have a constructive argument with someone who couldn't remember what happened and couldn't remember why he didn't remember what'd happened.

I was exhausted by trying to make sure Peter's epilepsy medication was taken regularly and at the correct dose. But my efforts were ineffective as evidenced by the number of double-doses and no-doses that occurred; he was clever at hiding doses that he said he'd taken and saving them up to double-dose. After all, he didn't think there was anything wrong with him. The outcome was that Peter was either having more seizures than he should have or was asleep for a couple of days after too much medication.

The husband I had said goodbye to when he left for work on 11 November was no longer the same man. I felt numb and sad for both of us.

Years later, when I completed the Total Strength Deployment Inventory (SDI) developed by Elias Porter[1], I discovered that my strength of tolerance was somewhat overdone when things were going well and also when I faced conflict. The SDI is a psychometric test based on relationship awareness theory and it helped me understand my motivation and related behaviour when things were going well and when faced with conflict.

---

1   https://en.wikipedia.org/wiki/Elias_Porter

In taking a Total SDI assessment[2] I discovered that my strength of tolerance was somewhat overdone when things were going well and also when I was faced with conflict.

I was paralysed for a long time by my patience and tolerance for my situation. I was so sorry for Peter and what he was going through. When people came to visit him, they were glad to see him alive. His head was shaved, and he had a large wound from one ear across the top of his head to the other ear. I also was grateful he was still alive, and I tolerated everything else that wasn't normal.

When Jason was three months old, we all moved back to our own house. Life was 'ordinary' for a long time. I couldn't work, and Peter couldn't work. Dad was desperately sorry for Peter and also struggled to keep the business going without his top salesman. Mum was a machine – cooking, nurturing, calming, working, and giving fantastic support to me. Progress came. Peter's speech returned, and he was able to walk steadily. But the changes to his personality and executive functioning were permanent. That's when I realised this wasn't a severe illness from which he would recover.

My husband would never again meet expectations within the family business. I would be driving and always on alert for the glazed look that precipitated his seizures. We tried to live a 'normal' life as much as possible, but the load between us was unequal.

Jason became an adorable toddler and then a child full of energy with a great personality. It was loads of fun. I devoted myself to being the best mum I could be and giving him the best family life we could have. But those attempts often seemed to be thwarted.

---

2   https://totalsdi.com/

We had planned a weekend in Launceston, staying at a motel with a great playground. Peter and Jason, then aged 2, went to the playground while I had a shower. As I was drying my hair, I heard ambulance sirens, but I paid no attention to them until they got closer, then stopped. I ran out of the motel room to see Peter on the ground, having had a seizure at the top of the slide where he'd played with his son. Jason was in the arms of a stranger.

Another day, we went to a family barbecue on a Sunday afternoon. When I was driving us home, Peter went into a seizure, leaned over, and grabbed the steering wheel. I don't know where I got the strength from to keep the car on the road until I could safely pull over.

One day at Kmart, Peter was pushing Jason in the trolley while I browsed. Peter had a seizure. Once again, I don't know where I got the strength from to keep the trolley upright and prevent Jason from falling out, while at the same time breaking Peter's fall to the ground.

After his seizures, Peter felt tired for the entire next day. For me, the impact was also huge — fear, adrenaline, raised cortisol, and reinforcement of my natural anxious state. No one else understood what I was going through. When I told others about the seizures, they would respond, 'Oh, well. He's okay now.' That was debatable, and I sure as hell was not okay.

Our second child, Alanna, arrived in September 1986. The perfect little sister and daughter; we all loved her. I became sensitive to their safety, perhaps intensified by hormones and an increased level of responsibility with a nearly 5-year-old and a baby.

Peter had smuggled cigarettes into our home, hidden them, and smoked them in the middle of the night. I'd woken one morning to a smouldering lounge. On other occasions there were burns in the carpet. Several times, I found smoking hot oil in the deep fryer that he'd abandoned, again in the middle of the night. Peter drove with Jason in the car, despite being told that he was not fit to drive. He would often double-dose his medication, leaving him with no ability to function for several hours.

Another time, Alanna was sleeping in the bassinet on the floor in the lounge room. Peter lost his balance and fell on top of her. Fortunately, he didn't hurt the 3-week-old Alanna, but she was screaming and scared, and so was I. I was anxious and fearful because of his severe epilepsy.

I realised the impact of what had happened to us because of Peter's illness. I later came to understand this as my unexpected crap-hand. But at the time, I knew that platitudes from others didn't help. Often, I heard, 'Oh, that's a shame. He loves Jason and Alanna, and they love him. He's a good bloke. It will be okay. You'll be alright.' But I gradually realised the full scale of the unexpected crap-hand that was dealt to me, to Peter, the children, to us as a family and our future. No amount of tolerance would fix it or keep us safe.

There I was, stunned into a realisation that I had to make some changes, and at the start of a long journey of recovery from my unexpected crap-hand.

What I know now is this: life-changing, unexpected, and unfortunate circumstances can affect anyone at any time. It happened to me. Perhaps it has happened to you. My experience put me into a place I didn't want to be. But I was powerless to move. I didn't know how to move. I was terrified. I was stuck.

At some point in your life, you may need to find a way to deal with a situation or circumstance that has taken you beyond the normal.

I'll tell you how I define the unexpected crap-hand in the next pages. For now, you might recognise these feelings: you are full of fear or feel no confidence. You think you have no experience dealing with unexpected crap-hands. Perhaps you don't know that such a hand exists. But through the journey of dealing with it consciously, you will discover you have resilience muscles you didn't know you had. You will also realise that you have formed resilience muscles from other events and moments in your life. All of these moments are moments to learn from and they are so valuable.

In 2019, a post on social media caught my eye. It said, 'One day you'll tell your story of how you overcame what you went through. And it will be someone else's survival guide.' This post motivated me to tell my story in public for the first time, at a conference, in October of that year. When I heard from attendees that they were inspired and strengthened by my story, I started to revive a long-held plan to write a book about it.

An unexpected crap-hand defined

After reading my story, you might think, 'Wow, that's a hard experience for her to have gone through. My experience doesn't compare.' Or perhaps you are thinking, 'My unexpected crap-hand is so much worse than that.'

I have found that determining what makes a crap-hand is a personal judgement. I'll give you a definition of what makes for an unexpected crap-hand, but a big part of determining if you have been dealt one or not is how you apply this definition. I know that something from my story will help you find the steps to move in a positive direction from whatever unexpected issue or challenge you are dealing with — even if it does not fit my definition.

What is an unexpected crap-hand? Let me say, it's not a technical term. It's a term I use to describe my experience. I do not mean to trivialise my experience or yours with this slightly glib description. For me, the term helps me put my life's tragedies into perspective and escape self-pity. It's not a term that I used at the time, but I started to use it much later as I began to assemble my ideas for this book.

There are three principles you can use to define an unexpected crap-hand. The first principle is that it's a life-changing adverse event. It might be an accident, a health crisis, or something else. It is a loss, and it is a shock. Whatever it is, it significantly changes something about your life.

The second principle is that there's no obvious fix. No matter how you think about your problem, the solution is not straightforward or easy.

The third principle is that only you know how bad it is. That's where the personal judgement comes in. It doesn't matter what another person thinks about your experience.

If you believe that you have experienced a life-changing and adverse event, where there is no obvious fix, and only you know how bad it is, then it fits my definition to be an unexpected crap-hand.

Life events happen all the time:

- a miscarriage

- a small-business failure
- a serious car accident
- a fifth unsuccessful IVF cycle.

You might consider them unexpected crap-hands, or not, depending on how you choose to apply my definition.

But they are awful situations to go through. You experience feelings of loss and lack of control, and of being trapped, frustrated, and unsuccessful. You might feel sad or depressed.

Do a quick Google search, and you'll find lots of tips to deal with unforeseen circumstances. Suggestions include things like:

- Have a positive attitude.
- Don't get angry.
- Build your inner strength.
- Keep control of yourself and focus on the present.

However, these tips are of limited value. They're probably not appropriate for the situations described above. They are certainly not robust enough for you to use when dealing with the type of unexpected crap-hand as I define it.

I don't want to downplay any of the examples I've given above. They're all situations we'd rather not experience. But there is another type of life event: it's got an added dimension to it. It's when a terrible event *happens to someone close to you*:

- Your spouse has a miscarriage.
- Your parent is killed in a car accident.
- Your business partner dies in a fire.
- Your life partner is diagnosed with a terminal illness.

These events have a devastating impact on your life and the lives of those around you. No matter how hard you try to fix it or run away from it, you can't. It's there, it's in your face, and only you know how bad it is. There is no doubt – that is an unexpected crap-hand.

As well as your grief and confusion, you are in a swirling sea of emotions and consequences. You are drowning with the weight of being responsible for making decisions on behalf of others. You are just so sad for others that are affected. This is where I found myself. This is why my unexpected crap-hand – the illness of my husband – had such a profound effect on me and others around me.

You are unique. Nobody has the lived experience that you do. No one knows how good or bad things are for you. There are all sorts of circumstances that contribute to the depth of goodness or badness about your life.

You'll notice that others react in different ways. Every reaction is influenced by people's prior experiences, the mood of the day, and their level of empathy and compassion. But at the end of the day, only you know how bad it is and how far-reaching the consequences are. And you feel alone.

One way to look at the difference between a bad hand and an unexpected crap-hand is to think about the weight of one compared with the other.

A significant part for me was that it was *my* issue. No one else could understand what I was experiencing. No one else knew how bad it was. I had to dig deep to do something. I also wanted to keep everyone happy. With the wisdom of experience and age, I know now that that is impossible – and not necessary. That desire, however, added a layer of complexity as I tried to navigate through it.

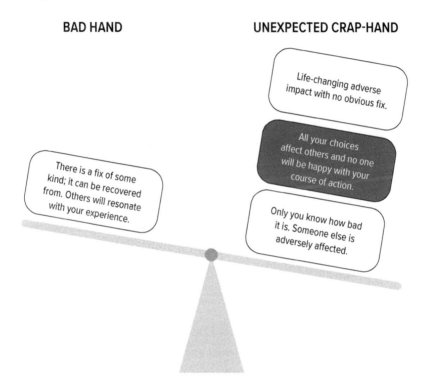

BAD HAND

UNEXPECTED CRAP-HAND

Life-changing adverse impact with no obvious fix.

All your choices affect others and no one will be happy with your course of action.

There is a fix of some kind; it can be recovered from. Others will resonate with your experience.

Only you know how bad it is. Someone else is adversely affected.

I concluded that you're facing an unexpected crap-hand when everything has changed for the worse, and you can't see an obvious fix. You're having a bad time on a level that people can't understand or perhaps they don't dare to empathise with, because if they say, 'How are you?' the tears will never stop. No matter how you look at it, you cannot see a way out where everyone will be happy.

Here's a scenario that demonstrates the difference between a bad hand and an unexpected crap-hand. You go out for dinner at a restaurant. Your partner is pregnant. You both get food poisoning and are in hospital for three days. You both need two weeks off work to recover. No one else in the restaurant gets food poisoning. That's a bad hand.

Same scenario. You go out for dinner, and you both get food poisoning. The bug is listeria. The baby is born at 26 weeks. While the baby survived, he will have lifelong health issues as a result.

I provided three principles earlier of an unexpected crap-hand.

And one or more of the criteria below might apply. If so, I'd say that you have experienced an unexpected crap-hand if:

- you or someone else will never recover full physical or mental health
- a relationship is irretrievably changed or broken
- all your choices leave people feeling unhappy or negatively affected.

There will be something in this book that you can use for every adverse circumstance in life. You can define if it's a bad hand or an unexpected crap-hand. Or somewhere in between. Only you know.

For nearly five years, I was not aware that I had been dealt an unexpected crap-hand. I just kept going. I was determined to make every day as right as it could be. I was becoming dissatisfied with the situation and worried, but I don't remember ever describing it as or thinking about it as a devastating life event. In recent years, I've discovered so much about myself, which points to the possible reasons why I didn't think of it in that way. Some of them might apply to you too.

I hold an overdone strength of tolerance. Like all of us, I am the product of childhood conditioning, limiting beliefs, low self-image, low confidence, guilt, and shame. I also had an innate and irrational determination that I could fix these things. You may have similar thoughts. I now know that humans are hard-wired to put confidence before reality. There will be more about that in Chapter Six.

At this point, you might be realising that you have been dealt a hand that you want to recover from. And you might be scared to tackle what you need to do to get unstuck from where you are.

Dealing with an unexpected crap-hand is hard to navigate, and you do need motivation to sustain your efforts. Everyone's motivation will be different. For me, the motivation to do things differently came from the cumulative effect of many moments. Those moments started with me being concerned for the safety of my children, over some time, and culminated when Peter fell on top of Alanna in her bassinet.

After nearly 5 years of feeling unsafe and trying to manage challenging behaviours, I needed to stop procrastinating and solve a huge problem. I didn't want to admit that it was time to do something different. I could no longer persist with fear. I had a nearly 5-year-old and a 5-week-old baby.

When I weighed up the pros and cons, I needed to make a move in the interests of all of us. But I was so conflicted. He was a good bloke with an acquired brain injury. Peter loved the children so much. He would not want to be responsible for hurting them. He had been dealt an unexpected crap-hand too.

The final moment came one Friday afternoon. I was exhausted. I lay on the bed and fell asleep. I woke to some clanging and clunking on the front stairs that passed by the bedroom window. It was Peter dragging the pram up the stairs. The baby was in the pram. She was 5 weeks old. There were no blankets, no protection from the sides of the pram and she was bumping up against the framework of the pram. There was a way to remove the bassinet from the pram and carry it upstairs, but Peter couldn't process that thinking. I could bear it no longer.

Around midnight that night, I was lying in bed with my son and daughter in the middle of the bed, in her cocoon. The reality of them not being safe hit me harder than ever before.

There is a saying, 'No mud, no lotus.' It means that the challenge itself brings on the challenge to cultivate inner attributes.

It was then I realised I had a choice. I could make decisions, and suddenly, I realised I had a goal – to keep us safe. Tony Robbins[3] says that setting goals is the first step in turning the invisible into the visible. While I didn't know about Tony Robbins back then, he is so right.

There is a Greek word 'praxis' which is the integration of your beliefs with your behaviour. This was what I needed to do. I struggled, but the quest for the common good prevailed. In this case, the common good was the protection of all of us. I didn't want the children to be hurt. I didn't want to be hurt. I didn't want Peter to do something that would hurt us without meaning to. He would have hated that. While I had resisted the solution for so long, it became clear that the problem I'd been terrified about was more dangerous than the solution. The problem was that I didn't think we were safe. The solution was to find the way to keep us safe.

---

3   https://www.facebook.com/TonyRobbins/posts/setting-goals-is-the-first-step-in-turning-the-invisible-into-the-visible-the-fo/10154503990719060/

I confess to not having seen my situation in this simple way before. I was more preoccupied with coping with my loss rather than figuring out what the future needed to look like. I remember the doctor who delivered my son saying to me, at my six-week check-up, that 'Everyone has a cross to bear.' This was another moment that reinforced what I'd heard when growing up: you make your bed and you need to lie in it. But I now knew that I had to find a way to live away from Peter, with the children. I was almost there, but I hadn't reached the key to change, my tipping point.

Then I drowned in emotion. For a moment, the path had seemed clear. Reality set in – there were consequences to what I was going to do. But I did have one foot on the path. I had a goal, and the goal was safety for all.

Now you have heard about the event in my life that has been the catalyst for personal development that I have applied across all parts of my life.

With the desire to help others deal with situations where they feel stuck, I've developed a model to guide these changes. My model involves grit – the positive, well-intentioned grit that forms when you have a focus and a plan for the future.

That grit is conscious grit.

Conscious grit will get you unstuck.

Staying in conscious grit and developing skills and confidence will make you unstoppable.

CHAPTER TWO

It's a gritty world

*Step out of the history that is holding you back. Step
into the new story you are willing to create.*

— Oprah Winfrey

Grit

In this chapter I take you into the world of grit. The kind of grit that
will get you unstuck, or as Oprah Winfrey says, into the new story
you are willing to create.

We all know about one kind of grit. If you go to the beach for the
afternoon, you will find grit in your car, between your toes and
maybe in your bed!

There is another form of grit. The personal traits that are often
characterised by bravery, spirit, courage, consistency, toughness,
tenacity, and strength and passion. You may have heard people
label others by saying, 'He or she is really gritty.' Being gritty is a
positive state – unless it's overdone.

Gritty people tend to believe that everything will be okay eventually, and if it's not okay, then it's not the end. And they just continue. The word 'yet' is an important word to them. They keep going because they are not there 'yet', but they know that they want to get to a particular way of being or living or behaving or relating.

My model includes two types of grit. Neither is bad, but one type will help you have a better life.

There is unconscious grit. This is the grit that will help you survive in a difficult situation. It is the kind that can also keep you stuck in managing a problem in a particular way.

There is conscious grit. This is the grit that can get you out of the problem, the grit you need to get unstuck. It is the grit that you need to live your best life.

Life isn't easy. We're all faced with situations in our lives where we have to manage events, whether in our professional or personal lives. If we manage those events passively, we're not going to live a life that we want to live. Even if you haven't had an unexpected crap-hand, you will have had some incident, issue, or problem that kept you awake at night – at the very least. There will be an issue that needs a gritty approach to deal with it.

When you look around your family and friends, you'll see all sorts of things that people are dealing with. You will notice relationship issues, serious accidents, terminal illnesses, people providing support to the elderly, the consequences of unemployment and poverty, drug and alcohol issues, and housing issues.

They may be dealing with those challenges with unconscious or conscious grit.

Have you ever been for a drive and you go for kilometres over dusty, unsealed roads with potholes, bumps, and ditches? The roadsides are overgrown with weeds, and dust gets into your vehicle even if you have the windows up. You keep going. It's not pleasant. Sometimes you want to stop or pull over and hope that someone comes along and shows you an easier way. But they don't come. Each pothole you hit tells you repeatedly, in that awful loop of self-talk that we get into sometimes, 'I am a failure. People think I'm hopeless. I don't know what to do. I'll just have to hang in there. There are no other options, and no one else understands. I'll just put up with it. I'm scared.' You try your best to put up with the dust and potholes. You display tenacity and determination as you go. When you get home, the car is dirty, and bugs are stuck to the windscreen. This is what being in the zone of unconscious grit is like.

Then you reach a part of the road that's paved with bitumen, and it's grey. It's not pretty, but at least it's a smoother ride. When you come to an intersection, you have awareness and the ability to choose which way you will go. You are less prone to listen to the negative voices in your head. You start to think more clearly, you're doggedly persistent, and you're able to choose responses that will serve you well. In this state, you have a plan and the ability to move from fear to action, which takes courage. This is being in the zone of conscious grit.

When you read my story, the evidence is compelling. I had a problem. I dealt with it in a persistent, tenacious, determined, and resilient way. I had 'little c' courage. But I still had a problem, and I was stuck. I did a great job because I had two beautiful children and a lovely little home but few prospects for a fulfilling life (based on my definition of what that was). You will have your own definition. When I added a couple of other elements – future focus and planning, I moved into the zone of conscious grit. That was how I got unstuck.

I didn't know it at the time, but what I do know now is that while I was in each of the zones and then moving between them, I was learning, developing and gaining skills that I didn't have before. I learned about myself and about others. My confidence grew and my knowledge and ability to find out what I needed to know improved dramatically. I was building, scaffolding and leveraging from everything I tried – whatever the outcome. I was learning what worked and what didn't work.

Like most things in life there are various shades, intensities, grades of good, bad and better. It's no different with grit. I know I live in the zone of conscious grit these days, but there are still some days when I am not in the sweet spot. I'm still in the zone – I haven't hopped back into the zone of unconscious grit. I'm just on the edge of conscious grit.

This thing called life that we are navigating is complex and dynamic and far from perfect. It's reasonable to be 'in the zone' rather than in a perfectly neat package tied up with a bow and a label that says conscious grit.

Your aim is to get into the zone of conscious grit and then to stay there. We are all human. If you drift over the edge of the zone into unconscious grit, you will know from this book to recognise the signs and how to navigate back.

Unconscious grit

When you are in the zone of unconscious grit, you are trying hard. You are displaying a determination to hang in there. You have a day-to-day focus, and you make the best of the situation as though you are coping with the struggle, even when you think that you can't deal with it. You haven't given up; you're just beavering away to do what's instinctively right. You are courageous to a point. It's a 'little c' courage that helps a bit. But you need more. You don't have a plan and you don't have a future focus.

I didn't know when managing life after Peter's illness that I was in the zone of unconscious grit. At the time, I was just determined to do the best I could, simple as that. Years later, when trying to make sense of my life, this concept of unconscious grit was constructed. It's vital to know that you are in the zone of unconscious grit. When you know it, you can decide to move out of it. It's worth moving out of it. It's unlikely you will reach your potential if you stay in that zone.

My experience of being in the zone of unconscious grit can be compared to swimming in treacle. It's too hard to move. You can't leave the treacle behind, and it sticks with you. It presents as sickly sweet, but it's toxic. Each day is the same sticky slog of good intention.

It can also be compared to 'spinning your wheels'. There's so much energy going into creating the momentum, and it keeps the wheels turning fast, but no progress is made. The scenery is the same, day after day.

I also align the experience to carrying water in a sieve. I was trying my best, but there was no way I was going to succeed. It's frustrating and demoralising.

Don't get me wrong. People in the zone of unconscious grit are trying extremely hard. They are determined, tenacious, persistent, resilient, have 'little c' courage within them, and have an 'I can fix it' attitude. They are doing an excellent job for the here and now, but it's a focus that is about everyone else. They have given up thinking about themselves. And they have lost sight of the concept of maximising their potential.

People in the unconscious grit zone don't know what to do to change the circumstances that they need to change. They do know they will make the best of whatever circumstances they are in. They are gritty. They might go it alone and not tell anyone because they don't want others to know how bad the reality is. They keep busy and do all the right things to keep life on an even keel. In secret, they hope that someone will notice and throw them the key to escape.

If they choose to stay in the unconscious grit zone, they will be missing out on a better life. It's that simple.

From my story, you will see that I muddled around in the zone of unconscious grit for an extended period. It wasn't all bad, but I was able to develop a better life when I made a deliberate move into a different zone. This is the zone I now call the zone of conscious grit.

I know that when I was in the unconscious grit zone, I was doing a 'good job'. But it wasn't going to be enough to keep us safe. Further, while I was focused on keeping us safe, it was hard to find energy and space to focus on other things.

In the zone of unconscious grit:

- I had no qualifications
- my only aspiration was to keep us safe
- I was scared and safety was always on my mind
- I was reasonably isolated (by my choice I now realise)
- I lost my partner – I was alone in any decisions I made.

Observers would have seen a mum who was committed to her children. My actions in moving away from Peter have troubled me over the years. But it wasn't right for me to stay in that way of life.

I was tired, exhausted, doing my best, feeling unsafe and had no plan for the future. I was determined, resilient, persistent and tenacious. I had 'little c' courage, but I wasn't getting anywhere. I was stuck.

Do you relate to any of the characteristics, behaviours and internal dialogues that are hallmarks of being in the zone of unconscious grit?

Characteristics of being in the Zone of Unconscious Grit	Behaviours used when in the Zone of Unconscious Grit		Internal dialogue repeated when in the Zone of Unconscious Grit
Determined Persistent Tenacious Have 'little c' courage Resilient	You are: Not maximising your full potential Applying effort to do your best Not realising you can be your own champion Just doing it to get it done On automatic pilot Rarely if ever sharing the load Too busy surviving to realise and appreciate what you are learning	Over-tolerant just to keep the peace Trying is important to you but you are afraid to fail Day-to-day focus Limited evidence of planning past the day to day You don't seek advice often, if at all Giving up is not an option	I can't I won't I'm scared It's MY responsibility It's MY mess, I'll fix it by myself

Stuck in unconscious grit

If you are stuck in the zone of unconscious grit, you will feel that you are in a rut. When in a rut, you can't or don't plan for the future. You're on autopilot. You're still doing a great job and trying hard; you're just in a place where you are not moving. This is being stuck in the zone of unconscious grit. We shouldn't judge how others are reacting to their circumstances, but we do.

How often have you heard yourself say things like, 'I don't know why she stays with him. I don't know why he puts up with her putdowns. I don't know why they work there; they're so unhappy.' I'm sure you've said it about yourself, 'I can't lose weight, save money, or move jobs.'

In the community, some people will be stuck for other reasons. Sadly, there are lots of adults and children living with family violence. In the workplace, there will always be personality conflicts, petty fallings out, and rudeness. Some people can be damaged by continuing to work in toxic work environments. If you are a person that is justifying why it's okay for you to be stuck, remember that your situation is just for this moment. If you want to change things, you can.

If you doubt the impact of staying stuck for some time, consider this. Imagine you're holding a glass of water. If you hold it for a minute, it's not a problem. If you hold it for an hour, you'll have an ache in your arm. If you hold it for a day, your arm will feel numb and paralysed. The weight of the glass doesn't change but the longer you hold it, the heavier it becomes. The stresses and worries in life are like that glass of water. The more you hold them, the worse they will affect you.

In the next chapter I will tell you how I became unstuck. I needed validation. You might need that too. Or there may be other reasons why you're stuck. You might recognise them. Here are some.

- Unresolved issues might be keeping you stuck

Part of the conditioning from my childhood was repeatedly hearing that 'Good things come to those who wait.' There's a variation on that quote which makes more sense to the Gail of today, the Gail with the growth mindset, the Gail who knows how to get unstuck and the Gail who can't bear the thought of not having a plan and not making progress. That new phrase is, 'Good things happen to those who wait but better things come to those who go out and get them.'

Author and poet Emily Maroutian[4] says it well:

> You're not stuck. You're just committed to certain patterns of behaviour because they helped you in the past. Now those behaviours have become more harmful than helpful. The reason why you can't move forward is that you keep applying an old formula to a new level in your life. Change the formula to get a different result.

- Procrastination was my enemy – it might be yours too

One of the critical things that will hold you back from moving from the unconscious grit zone to the conscious grit zone is procrastination. My journey on that path was long – nearly five years – and I realise now that I was drowning in procrastination. In later and wiser years, I recognised that procrastination is among the most common reasons for motivational failure. Procrastination

---

4   https://www.goodreads.com/author/quotes/3496824.Emily_
     Maroutian?page=4

is associated with adverse states and problems, including increased stress, regret, and suffering. We use procrastination to avoid tasks that we don't want to do because we want to prevent negative feelings and more stress in our lives.

Multiple factors held me — an unpleasant task, anxiety, and loss aversion. Once you know what's stopping you, mobilisation is possible. The saying 'You can't steer a parked car' is relevant.

Years ago, I attended a conference and couldn't reconcile one of the topics with my thinking. I wrote an article on the way home on the plane about how it was troubling me. The article was later published in *Campus Review*. I think the uncomfortable feeling was the same feeling as procrastinating when I was in the zone of unconscious grit. That feeling where you know something is not quite right. You don't know what the answer is. You just know that you have to find it.

Remember the princess and the pea fairytale? In the story, the princess sleeps on an ever-increasing pile of mattresses, but can still feel the pea underneath the mattresses as an irritant. That was me for a long time — a princess in the zone of unconscious grit.

Operating in the zone of unconscious grit is not a great way to live. I knew I was going through something extremely uncomfortable. It was different from what my friends and relatives were going through. Though I tried to make sense of it, I couldn't, so I just dealt with it somehow, which is what you do in the zone of unconscious grit. I lived in fear of tackling, head-on, the aftermath of Peter's illness. I did have persistence, resilience, determination, and tenacity, but it was grit that just kept me churning in the moment for all of those days, hours, and minutes over nearly five years. I had 'little c' courage and was determined to make the best of the situation. But there was no projecting into, or planning for, the future.

When living day to day in the zone of unconscious grit, I lost sight of skills or capabilities that might have taken me forward. Like the hamster on the wheel, I was running in circles but making no progress. I was reactive, burning heaps of energy and getting nowhere fast. It was exhausting. I was exhausted because I could not find what I needed to get me off that wheel. Whenever I had a glimmer of a plan in my head, I sabotaged it by my internal dialogue that 'I just needed to put up with it.' These glimmers were quickly dimmed with a healthy dose of 'Others are not going to be happy with what I might need to do.'

In contrast, I wanted to succeed. After all, I had two little people and a husband who were also in a crap situation. I wanted to make it better for them. But I didn't know how to get mobile. I didn't know what success was.

There might be other reasons why you might not move out of the zone of unconscious grit. You may see the task as unpleasant, or anxiety might be a factor. You may not have explicit goals. You may not be able to see that there is a reward at the end. You may also be thinking that the present situation is more rewarding (or there is less opportunity to lose) if you stay in it. One of the instincts that humans have hard-wired into them is about avoiding loss. That is, we continue to invest in a bad situation rather than lose what we have already invested. Multiple factors held me: an unpleasant task, anxiety, and loss aversion. Could these be stopping you?

- Lack of validation

Lots of things get in the way of finding the motivation to make a move. In my case, and with the benefit of hindsight, at the heart of it was a lack of validation that I had a problem. My confidence was fragile. In my gut I knew I had a problem, but I needed to convince my head, my rational brain. When I received that, I did move. There will be more about this in Chapter Three.

- Fixed mindset

Mindset is so important. You might have a fixed mindset that's holding you back. If you say things like, 'I'm not creative. I'm a procrastinator. I've got nothing interesting to say. I can't learn now; it's too late. I'm not good at anything,' you have a fixed mindset. The good news is that you can change a fixed mindset into a growth mindset. There will be more on this in Chapter Three.

- Neglected mental health needs

When setbacks, trauma, or unexpected crap-hands happen, you experience waves of emotion like fear, anger, blame, and grief. Discomfort and uncertainty often follow. On reflection, I didn't deal with any of that at an emotional level. At the time of my unexpected crap-hand, I pressed on. My internal dialogue was – I could fix it. I could live with it. I'll be okay. It will be okay.

Years ago, there wasn't the positive focus on mental health that there is now. It was a taboo subject. The usual way to 'get over' any upset was 'to have a good cry'. We know now that there is more to maintaining positive mental health. Getting professional support to deal with trauma and emotional upheaval is important – and that is one critical part of looking after your mental health.

The first time I went to a psychologist was at least thirty years after the unexpected crap-hand. I went because we'd been burgled. We arrived home when the burglary was in progress. On that night, as I walked up our internal stairs, I felt there was something odd happening. There was a neat stack of laptop computers and other devices on our kitchen bench. When I entered our hallway, I could see that the windows in a bedroom were open. In another bedroom, drawers were upside down, and clothes had been disturbed. The culprits were on their way back for their second load, and we'd disturbed them.

Our house has a garage underneath, and after that event, when I came home from work, I would freeze in the car. I couldn't get out. The rational me was not able to convince the emotional me that we now had a security alarm that hadn't gone off, and that there was no one upstairs and inside.

At the appointment with the psychologist, I hardly talked about the burglary. I was drawn back to the unexpected crap-hand and its aftermath. I couldn't believe it. The psychologist explained that I hadn't dealt with the emotional trauma at the time. Thirty years later, my reaction to the burglary let me know that the original trauma needed to be dealt with. In hindsight, it's pretty obvious that, during the unexpected crap-hand, I hadn't reframed doubt, uncertainty, fear, anger, blame, and grief into a state that would serve me better.

Conscious grit

Looking back, I realise that there was a time when I shifted gear. I finally got some traction around the things I needed to do – keep safe, get some money, and develop a career. I started to do things differently. I know now that I was in the zone of conscious grit. In that zone:

- I made tough decisions
- I had tough conversations

- I set a course
- I stayed firm with the resolve of my direction
- I got qualifications, employment, and confidence to craft the future.

It's hard to move from the zone of unconscious grit. While I was there, I knew it was tough, but I thought I was doing okay. While I was in that zone for five years, that might not be true for you. You might be there for less or more time; there is no 'right' time frame. Every situation is different, and the fallout will be different. The risks will be different. The point here is that you do have a choice. It's up to you to choose whether you live in the zone of unconscious or conscious grit. There might be a sobering reality for you as there was for me. I will never regret making my choices, but I have had to work hard to reconcile my decisions. This may also be true for you.

When I moved into the zone of conscious grit, I added a focus on the future and planning, and maintained my determination, resilience, persistence and tenacity. My 'little c' courage became 'big C' Courage. I was still tired but had a plan to achieve our goal of safety. I felt less stuck. I was on the move.

I wasn't aware that if I added in some more planning and future focus, I would make progress. It can be tempting to stay in the zone of unconscious grit. As you keep reading this book, you will see that once you do move out of it, things get better — and they also get more complicated. However, in my case, the greater good was better served by being in the zone of conscious grit. I did see reward for effort. It would not have been fair to anybody for me to stay in unconscious grit. I couldn't keep us safe if nothing changed. The common good was apparent. I had only good intentions. The power of having a goal – safety – became a beacon and a light for the common good.

I used conscious grit to grow lemons.

In Tasmania, it's customary to have a lemon tree in your back garden. My parents had one that was always laden with lemons, and it was a source of great connection in our family. If you needed lemons, you would go and see Mum and Dad; they'd have some. I tried to grow a lemon tree, and it didn't grow. It lost its leaves, never had any fruit or blossoms, and the branches were sparse. I did all the things you do in unconscious grit. I paid attention to it, but in the same way I always had. I didn't try anything new. I was tenacious and determined with my watering, but it wouldn't grow.

My dad was an impressive gardener. When he died in 2018, I decided to focus on my underwhelming lemon tree. I wanted to prove that I could be some kind of gardener. I watered it by hand, used seaweed fertiliser, removed the damaged leaves, and then I watched as the trunk and the branches grew stronger. The leaves became greener and shinier, and there were more of them. Then buds formed on the branches and blossomed, and they grew and set. Then I had tiny little lemons. Then I had bigger lemons, and then I had a lemon on the kitchen bench. The first lemon I had ever grown. It wasn't a lemon like Dad grew; it was my lemon. I could feel the juiciness inside. I could smell the lemony-ness, and I loved the smooth yellow skin. I felt so satisfied.

This showed me many things. It taught me what happens when you use unconscious grit. You pay attention, but you just do what you've always done. And nothing changes.

Then when you use conscious grit, things change. I saw the potential and got motivated. I discovered that nurturing is good for you and whatever is being nurtured. I persisted and found that little actions do matter. In nurturing and persisting with my lemon tree, I learned that if you look for the signs, you'll know what to give — in this case, water or fertiliser. I was deliberate, I planned, and I was motivated. I wanted to prove that I could do what Dad did. Now I have the lemon tree, and I know the methods for getting it going and fruiting.

That was the benefit of shifting from the zone of unconscious grit to the zone of conscious grit to manage my lemon tree.

Create your toolbox

I have a metaphoric toolbox. It's old, painted dark red and has a few dents in it. Those dents represent the challenges that I've faced over the years. In it I've got lots of tools, tips and tricks that I've gathered. I'm going to give you some tools and personal projects throughout this book. You might want to store them in an imaginary toolbox, a big handbag, treasure chest, or old vintage suitcase. You might prefer to write them in a journal or put them on a sticky note on your wall. It doesn't matter how or where you store them, as long as you remember to use them when you need to.

Wherever you see this symbol in the book, there will be something to put into your toolbox.

Personal projects

Here are three Personal Projects. If you have a situation where you feel stuck, the personal projects will help you to:

- identify which zone you are in
- map your actions that will help you get unstuck
- identify what additional help you need to get unstuck.

Personal project 1: Which zone are you in?

Step 1: Think of a situation that you are trying to resolve. It might be as simple as my lemon tree challenge; it might be an unexpected crap-hand or somewhere in between. Use the table below to figure out which zone you are using for the situation you want to manage.

What situation are you wanting to manage? Write it here.					
	Tick the characteristics that you can relate to				
	The Zone of Unconscious Grit		The Zone of Conscious Grit		
Characteristics	Determination	☐	Determination	☐	
	Perseverance	☐	Perseverance	☐	
	Tenacity	☐	Tenacity	☐	
	'Little c' courage	☐	'Big C' Courage	☐	
	Resilience	☐	Resilience	☐	

Behaviours	You don't maximise your full potential	☐	You're determined to maximise your full potential	☐
	You use effort to do your best	☐	You use effort to do your best and have a plan and goals	☐
	You don't realise you can be your own champion	☐	You know you can be your own champion	☐
	You are on automatic pilot	☐	You're planned and purposeful	☐
	You just do it to get it done	☐	You plan to get it done in the best way possible	☐
	You have a day-to-day focus	☐	You have a day-to-day focus plus a future focus	☐
	There is limited evidence of planning past the day to day	☐	There is evidence of planning that has a future focus	☐
	You're over-tolerant to keep the peace	☐	You draw the line at what will be tolerated	☐
	If you try you might fail and that will bring shame	☐	If you try and it doesn't work out, you see it as a learning opportunity	☐
	You rarely, if ever, share the load	☐	You share the load often	☐
	You don't seek advice often, if at all	☐	You seek advice often, evaluate it and use it	☐
	You're too busy surviving to realise you are learning	☐	You look for learning opportunities when you manage the challenges	☐
	Giving up is not an option	☐	Giving up is not an option but you want to see changes and results as evidence of progress	☐
Metaphors	It feels like you're swimming in treacle	☐	It feels like you're swimming in water that continually changes, and you adapt to it	☐
	It feels like you're spinning your wheels	☐	It feels like you have traction	☐
	It feels like you're carrying water in a sieve	☐	It feels like you're carrying water in a leakproof container	☐

Internal dialogue	I can't	☐	I'll try	☐
	I won't		I can	
	I'm scared		I did it	
	It's MY responsibility		It's MY responsibility and I'm drowning under the weight of it. Can you help me?	
	It's MY mess. I'll fix it by myself		It's MY mess. I wouldn't mind running my ideas to fix it past you.	

After completing this, do you think you are in the zone of unconscious grit or conscious grit?

Do you want to move into the zone of conscious grit? Read on! You can find an editable template at www.everywhensolutions. com.au/resources

Personal project 2: Shift the dial

If you have a situation that you want to change, write it down.

_____

_____

_____

Now think about this question. On a scale of 1 to 10, what is the negative impact on you and your life right now (1 = 'very little', and 10 = 'extremely negative')?

1	2	3	4	5	6	7	8	9	10
VERY LITTLE				MODERATE					EXTREME

Where do you want to move the negative impact on you after you've taken some action?

1	2	3	4	5	6	7	8	9	10
VERY LITTLE				MODERATE					EXTREME

Write down what you want to change, and what needs to change to move along the scale in the direction you want to.

_____

_____

_____

What criteria from the zone of conscious grit are you going to use? Write them down.

_____

_____

_____

Now write down three specific actions you are going to take to move your score on the dial to where you want it to be.

I am going to:

1. _____

2. _____

3. _____

That's a significant first step in taking action in dealing with whatever is going on for you. The action steps won't work unless you commit to writing them down. Then take action. I recommend you tell someone you trust and ask them to call you in four weeks to see if you are shifting the dial of your life – or still only thinking about what needs to happen. Perhaps something is keeping you stuck?

Personal project 3: Steps to help you get unstuck

First, decide on your commitment to getting unstuck. Which of these seven statements fits for you right now?

1. 'I **can't** get unstuck.'
2. 'I **hope** I can get unstuck.'
3. 'I **will try** to get unstuck.'
4. 'I **want to** get unstuck.'
5. 'I **will do the best** I can to get unstuck.'
6. 'I'm **doing the best** I can to get unstuck.'

7. 'I am **doing whatever it takes** to get unstuck.'

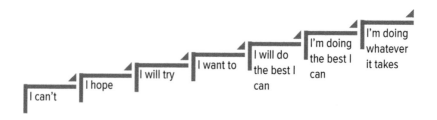

Ask yourself these questions at every step until you can move to the next one:

- What would it take for me to move to the next step?
- What's keeping me there?
- What do I need to do?
- Do I need professional help?
- What kind?
- Do I need to talk to someone with specialist knowledge?
- Do I need legal advice?
- A counsellor?
- What do I need to adopt from the behaviours, internal dialogue examples and characteristics of conscious grit?
- What am I going to do and by when?

You can use the editable worksheets on my website. www.everywhensolutions.com.au/resources

Moving between the zones

In my story there was a tipping point which was the key to me starting to operate in conscious grit. My internal dialogue shifted from 'I'll try to do it,' to 'I can do it.'

I began to recognise small successes and say, 'I did it.' The following table shows the feelings you may have at the time you are in each zone.

The Zone of Unconscious Grit persistent, determined, resilient, tenacious and using 'little c' courage		The Zone of Conscious Grit persistent, determined, resilient, tenacious and using 'big C' Courage about the here and now AND about the future and planning		
I can't – you might feel sadness	I'm scared – you might feel fear	I'll try – you might feel a sense of anticipation	I can – you might feel surprise	I did it – you might feel joy

I've recognised the steps in my behaviour in the first few years after Peter's illness. I knew I needed to find another way to manage the situation. My internal dialogue, however, was, 'I can't do it,' 'I'm scared to do it.' I was in the zone of unconscious grit. My internal dialogue was influenced by the primary emotional state of fear, a feeling that I lacked the ability or the competence to do what I needed to do in the way that I needed to do it, and a worry that others would think the worse of me.

I knew in my gut that I needed to do things differently, but I didn't change my approach for a long time. I needed to get to 'I'll try, I can, I did.'

In his book, *Authentic: How to Be Yourself and Why It Matters*, Stephen Joseph[5] says that to navigate life successfully to make the best decisions for yourself at any given moment, you need to be authentic. You need to counter external influences pulling you to go against the grain of your gut feelings.

Now I know that to be authentic is an excellent way to live. It's something that I aspire to every day in my wiser adult life. I didn't know how important it was back in the early to mid '80s. I didn't have the confidence, capabilities or skills to counter those external influences pulling me away from what my gut was telling me.

There will be an emotional journey that goes along with choosing to get to the zone of conscious grit. It accompanies any substantial life-changing decision. You can get wobbly. It may not look wonderful or even right, to begin with. At times it will haunt you and you may feel overwhelmed and helpless. This is when you draw on your tenacity, determination, persistence, resilience and 'small c' courage as you move towards your tipping point: the key to getting into the zone of conscious grit.

You might be thinking that the difference between the two zones is subtle, and there is not much difference. But there is a lot of difference. Think about my lemon tree. Had I not managed that tree with a future focus and some planning, it would have continued to struggle along with a life that wasn't the best. It is worth finding the 'big C' Courage (or gumption, as my mum would say), to get going and think about the future – to be in the zone of conscious grit.

---

5   Joseph, S 2016, *Authentic: How to be Yourself and Why it Matters*, Little, Brown Book Group, United Kingdom

None of us likes criticism, and sometimes external opinions will affect you, denting your confidence. You might hear from others 'What do you want to do that for?' 'Can't you just be satisfied with what you've got?' 'He/she won't cope if you do that.' You might even hear 'You are so selfish.' In Chapter Four, I will tell you about a tool that you can use to help you withstand such comments.

I have a sign hanging outside my office, and it says, 'Behind every successful woman is herself.' It was given to me by two special people, and it reminds me to remember – in a challenging situation, the only thing I can control is me. It reminds me not to wait for someone else to take action to change my situation, but to get moving at the pace that's right for me at the time. It reminds me to make the judgements and choices that are right for me.

Be inspired by Lauren.

She had been in a relationship for eight years. She and her partner bought a house. Two years later, the relationship was over. She was hurt, sad, and thought that no one would love her again. He wanted the house sold. She tapped into her savvy financial thinking, dug in her heels, withstood the pressure to comply with a sale, did her homework, and took a future focus. He said he'd be happy with quite a bit of cash; she negotiated a more reasonable offer than was on the table. In the zone of unconscious grit, she wouldn't have had the 'big C' Courage to take a future focus to drive her response. Lauren, however, was in the zone of conscious grit, and she reaped the benefits.

In speaking with Lauren, I know she didn't jump from the zone of unconscious grit to the zone of conscious grit in one big, neat step. She got onto the path gingerly and tested it out. She felt the difference. Something she couldn't put her finger on shifted. She noticed an upward swing in mood, and she noticed little steps of moving forward. She approached conversations with trepidation and yet still found confidence to push through.

CHAPTER THREE

Find your tipping point into the zone of conscious grit

'Go back?' he thought. 'No good at all! Go sideways? Impossible! Go forward? Only thing to do! On we go!' So up he got, and trotted along with his little sword held in front of him and one hand feeling the wall, and his heart all of a patter and a pitter.

— JRR Tolkien, *The Hobbit*

Tipping points can be elusive

In Chapter One, you read that I needed to find a way for the children and me to live in a safe way — and, sadly, that was not with Peter. I'd tried and failed.

Later in this chapter, I will tell you how I had a life-changing conversation with a doctor. I was by now **28** years old. It was a conversation where I moved into the zone of conscious grit. To do this I needed to find my tipping point. It happened before my eyes, when I didn't know that it was happening. But like the Hobbit, with my heart all of a pitter patter, I continued on. And then it happened.

The tipping point will show up differently for each of us. It might be a metaphoric tap on the shoulder, or it might be a real or metaphoric shove onto a different path. It might be someone's gentle persuasion or someone's sharp words. The common thing, though, is that it's the moment of truth when you can no longer ignore your pain. In this time of profound change, you know that your pain can no longer be tolerated. You commit to doing things in a different way. You can no longer ignore the knot in your stomach or the feeling that you have a hole in your heart. You can't ignore the overwhelming feeling that you need to change direction. My tipping point was the start of a life-changing experience.

You may not relate to the term 'tipping point'. If not, insert any of the following. In the context of the point I am making they are all the same: turning point, trigger point, the key, defining moment, moment of truth, crossroad, watershed moment, game changer, pivotal point.

At the tipping point, something happens to mobilise you into taking a different direction or approaching a problem in a different way. The tipping point comes when there is an event (a meeting, conversation, you read a powerful book, see a counsellor) AND one or more of the following happens:

- You recognise someone as a lifeline.
- You recognise yourself or someone else as a champion of your cause.
- You gain validation or affirmation.
- Your rational brain tells you that you must commit to doing things differently.

- Your heart tells you that you must do things differently.
- Your gut, or intuition, consistently niggles you and you know that things need to be different.

I call these the keys to tipping into the zone of conscious grit. You need to catch the tipping point when it's in your realm.

Then you 'tip' into conscious grit. When you have moved into conscious grit, you will notice some internal changes. Possible actions that seemed impossible in the past now seem more palatable. Actions to be taken are clearer. Your energy levels rise, and you can't ignore that you are going to act in a different way. You start seeing the situation in a different way. You do things differently from here on. All the qualities you demonstrated up to this point – being determined, persistent, resilient, tenacious and acting with 'little c' courage – continue. Plus, you get excited about having a plan and a future focus. You stand firm on that future focus and will be considering options that you would never have thought possible.

It was the start of a transition period for me and others and was loaded with supercharged emotions of fear, anxiety and grief. At the same time, I had a surge of affirmation and confidence. For me, it was a feeling that right here, right now, I was suddenly driven, focused and committed to living a different life and that I was worthy of it.

Finally, I understood that I was important, that I needed to treat myself well and that if I didn't look after myself, I was not much use to others. I also realised that I was the only one who could look after myself. I got 'big C' Courageous from that point and considered options that I would never have previously considered. I began to live in the zone of conscious grit. And I started the journey of becoming unstuck.

Each of the following scenarios is a practical example of the events that led to tipping points and shows how circumstances can change once you are in the zone of conscious grit.

Meet Bonnie, mum of new baby.

Bonnie has a new baby who will not settle and cries for days and weeks. It has been suggested by her family and friends that she get some professional help to establish his routine. Bonnie has resisted. One day, she sits on the floor of the shower, exhausted, and accepts that she needs to reach out for the help she's been resisting. When she emerges from the shower, Bonnie realises that toddler Henry woke from his nap and got out of bed. He's covered in jam. She slumps to the floor and sobs. That's a tipping point.

She decides she will be the champion of managing the situation with commitment and persistence, tenacity and determination, and a plan. Bonnie moves into the zone of conscious grit. She finds 'big C' Courage and phones up her friends and family and tells them she is exhausted. Bonnie also tells them about the depths of her frustration and despair. She takes up the offers to babysit Henry. Bonnie trusts her inner voice that says she needs to go to the mother and baby unit for advice. In two months, the baby is settled with sound routines. Bonnie and Henry are enjoying their time together, enjoying the baby and not resenting him. Bonnie is more confident, and happier.

Meet Sam who is gaining weight.

Sam has been gaining weight for months and there has always been an excuse: it's the lead-up to Christmas or it's the holidays; it's the stress of going back to work or it's coming into winter. He knows he's been making excuses and that he would like to feel healthier. Sam finds out that he is on the cusp of diabetes.

That's a tipping point. He got the validation he needed to make a significant change.

Sam starts to think like a person in the zone of conscious grit. He finds out what changes are needed in his diet and exercise routine. He decides that buying less fast food will pay for the weekly subscription to a weight-loss support group. Sam tells a mate that he needs to go for a walk three times a week and asks him to keep him accountable as his champion. Courageously he tells his Thursday after-work drinking mates that he will only be popping in for one beer. He also tells them why. Sam makes another doctor's appointment for a month hence and is determined that the blood test in a month's time will show a shift in the right direction.

Meet Freya who is in a toxic work environment.

Freya's work environment is characterised by gossip, mixed messages, micromanaging and unconstructive criticism. Her values of authenticity, trust and honesty are often challenged. Her boss shuts her out of decisions for which Freya is responsible. Freya is committed to ensuring the project succeeds but her efforts are repeatedly undermined. Freya is publicly blamed for a decision that she wasn't involved in making. The decision significantly disrupts the project that she has been leading for eighteen months. She is embarrassed and feels powerless to correct the record. In the meantime, Freya hears that two of her colleagues are having time off work because of workplace bullying. They have completed incident reports about feeling unsafe.

When Freya becomes aware of this, she is at a tipping point; her colleagues have become her lifeline. Her experiences have been validated and affirmed by her colleagues' difficulties. In two weeks' time, after seeing no changes in her workplace, Freya puts her concerns in writing and pursues them with the human resources department. The department becomes her champion. Freya's mood shifts. She decides to leave the matter with HR and focuses on planning to get the best outcome for the project. She gets a surge of energy, determination, and tenacity.

Help-seeking

The serious nature of my situation was amplified when Peter fell into the baby's bassinet. It still took me a couple of weeks to act, but there was no coming back from that experience. My concerns about safety were constant and overwhelming. I'd resisted seeking help for so long. Help-seeking is a concept I had not heard of back then, but it's a well-researched area.

Organisations like Lifeline (www.lifeline.org.au/) have identified common barriers to help-seeking:

- You think the problem will go away by itself.
- You are too embarrassed or afraid to ask for help.
- You think you should be able to cope without help.
- You think things aren't bad enough to seek help.
- You don't know where to find help.
- There is a lack of support services.
- You think you'll be judged.
- You think help is too expensive or time-consuming.

For me, help-seeking was when I was motivated to go and talk to the family doctor. I made an appointment with him and told him how unsafe the situation was. I said, 'I don't know what to do.' His response was, 'You need to get a lawyer.' That was it. I had validation and affirmation. I had an independent person believing it was a situation that needed to change.

The decision was made, both in my head and in my heart. I just needed to do it. I had been thrown a metaphoric lifeline by the doctor. And when I grabbed onto it, I realised how much I had needed it. This quote by Marilyn Ferguson[6], author of *The Aquarian Conspiracy*, describes the feeling of living without a lifeline.

> *It's not so much that we are afraid of change or so in love with the old ways. But it's the place in between that we fear. It's like being between trapezes. It's Linus when his blanket is in the dryer. There's nothing to hold on to.*

That was a profound point in my life. I remember what I was wearing. On that afternoon dressed in my best matching track pants and top, and with children in tow, with sun streaming in through the window above the doctor's desk, I became my own champion.

I knew I had the commitment factor. After all, I had been committed to my family and to safety for nearly five years, hadn't I?

Now I had validation.

In summary, when I reflect on the model I've now created, this is what had happened to me:

- The doctor threw me a lifeline and I grabbed it.
- I became my own champion.
- I gained validation and affirmation that my challenge was real.
- I knew that I needed to do things differently – I was committed.

I admit it was then hard to take action.

---

6   https://www.goodreads.com/quotes/24386-it-s-not-so-much-that-we-re-afraid-of-change-or

Don't miss your potential tipping point

As with many parts of my journey, I didn't know what I didn't know until I knew it. I didn't know that a tipping point could be empowering.

I now know that tipping points are out there. They are swirling in the ether. And when we need one, we need to catch it.

When I caught my tipping point, I received validation. Before that, I didn't know that overt validation was so empowering. When I got it, I knew that I had needed it. It had been the missing part of my mental puzzle. I gained a sense of optimism and a strength that helped me know what I needed to do. It gave me additional motivation to do it.

However, although my position was validated, acting was still exceedingly difficult. It might not make sense to you, but whilst I had optimism and strength, I also had a sense of dread. My thoughts churned. What would everyone think? How could I do this to him? What sort of person does this to the person they married? On and on went the voices in my head.

But I did do what I needed to do; that's how I know that catching a tipping point is empowering.

While I was in the zone of unconscious grit, my determination, tenacity, persistence, resilience and 'little c' courage was used hour by hour every day. There is no doubt that I benefited from this enforced experience – as unpleasant as the circumstances were.

I learned lots in getting through every difficult day. I knew that I was competent – I could be mum, dad, teacher, listener, playmate, driver, organiser, provider, cook, cheerleader and fun maker – all at the same time if necessary. I'd become more confident. I was better equipped to know and act with 'big C' Courage, and to enable the tipping point when I got there.

I don't think you can predict where and when you might experience a tipping point. Maybe you won't even know that you've experienced it. But like many things in life, when you focus on them, they happen.

Remember Bonnie, Sam and Freya from the scenarios. They could all have let their situations continue – or deteriorate.

But they each treated the event as the key to catch a tipping point.

The same applies to my story. I could have stayed in the mode of avoiding seeking help – and never had the conversation. Or I could have ignored what the doctor said.

There's a hint in all of this – be alert for a tipping point!

Think about the following questions:

- Do you need to make a profound change in your life?
- Have you got your antennae up to 'catch' a tipping point?
- Can you be the champion? If not, who can be?
- Where is the likely lifeline?
- Do you have commitment?
- Where will you get your validation and affirmation from?
- What future focus and planning will you apply to your next moves?

Let's say you've recognised you're at a tipping point. You've figured out who can be your champion or lifeline. You know you have a commitment to doing things differently, and you have found validation and affirmation. You are now in the zone of conscious grit. When I got there, I saw the value of having a plan, setting goals and working towards them. There were still ups and downs, but overall I knew I was getting somewhere. Because I was making progress, I seemed to gather momentum. My self-esteem and confidence increased. Intuitively I know that I was on the right track with my decision-making and ability to problem-solve.

Here's a visual summary of how it works.

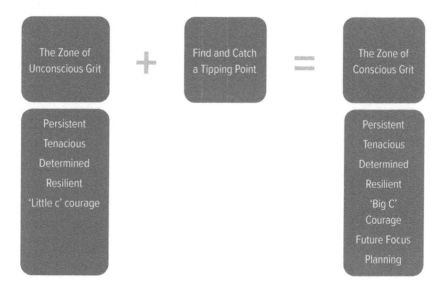

A warning

Be mindful that you might reach a tipping point and 'catch it' but the timing may not be right. That's why the future focus and planning components of being in the zone of conscious grit are important to use. If you need to manage safety or legal matters, then timing and sequencing in your plan are vital.

Catching the right tipping point is important. Planning for how you will act when in the zone of conscious grit is especially important.

Meet Mark.

Mark is a nurse who was injured by an aggressive patient. The processes for the work health and safety claim were demeaning, unfair, biased, lengthy and unsupportive. Surgery was required to repair his injury and Mark had months off work. The rehabilitation process was uncoordinated, and prolonged any settlement being made around the claim. Mark's immediate supervisor did not 'like' Mark. She was a bully to most of her team. She was never called to account for her behaviour.

Mark was in despair when his claim was denied by the insurance company. This could have been his tipping point. His immediate reaction was to resign. But Mark came across an old friend. He told him his story and the friend became his mentor. His tipping point was finding the mentor who affirmed that his claim was valid (in his view) and that bureaucratic meddling was the problem.

Mark added future focus and planning and decided that he could have a different reaction. He didn't want to give up the career he loved. He took some leave, got legal advice, pursued the claim, and won it. He returned to work. In the meantime, the supervisor had moved on (as often happens) and three years later, Mark is making the contributions as a nurse that he wants to.

Mark's story shows the value of catching the right tipping point.

PART TWO

CHAPTER FOUR

Goals and planning

Decide what it is you want.

Write that shit down

Make a plan

And...

Work on it.

Every.

Single.

Day.

— Author unknown

Setting goals to get you unstuck

Planning and having a future focus are key to being in the zone of conscious grit. When you get this right, your confidence increases and your desire to act with 'big C' Courage increases.

Setting goals is a crucial part of planning. When you have a goal, it will motivate you to do things differently.

Former First Lady Eleanor Roosevelt[7] said, 'It takes as much energy to wish as it does to plan.' Goal setting is empowering. It is a way to be intentional about creating the life you want. Setting goals will give you a sense of purpose and you will focus your energy and time on what's important to you. When you 'kick a goal', you are motivated to keep going and kick another goal.

The SMART model

The SMART model for setting goals was another one of those things that I didn't know about when I needed to know it. The model is a simple one. Goals need to be:

- S (specific) – think about what you want to achieve
- M (measurable) – decide how you will know when you've achieved it
- A (attainable) – consider if it is realistic and achievable
- R (relevant) – consider if it is relevant
- T (timely) – what's a realistic time to achieve it?

Here's a simple example.

Without using the SMART model
I want to lose some weight, maybe somewhere between 5 and 10 kg. But if I can't get my jacket done up in a couple of months, I'll just buy another one. I'm not sure what I'm going to change in my diet and exercise routine.

---

7   Eleanor Roosevelt Quotes (n.d.), *BrainyQuote.com*. Retrieved 22 November 2020, from https://www.brainyquote.com/quotes/eleanor_roosevelt_379411

Using the SMART model	
Specific	I want to lose 10 kg
Measurable	I want to lose 10 kg over the next six months
Attainable	Yes! I need to lose just under 400 g per week
Relevant	Yes, the doctors say it's a good idea, and I have a new jacket I will be able to do up
Timely	Yes, the time allocated is realistic. I can do this within six months.

Which approach do you think will work best?

Setting goals has served me well

I've applied the SMART model to my challenges retrospectively to show you how it worked (I didn't know I used a model at the time!).

- S = I needed to live with the children away from Peter.
- M = when it was done, it was done. When we had moved out, we had moved out, and I felt safe.
- A = it was achievable with lots of effort and planning.
- R = safety was at the core.
- T = it was going to take as long as it took. It was a big task after all!

Some years ago, I was looking to set ten-year goals as part of a leadership program. Through this program I had access to a life coach. I wanted to be a marriage celebrant and start a side gig that I might develop into a business when I retired, which was to be many years in the future. I was excited as I talked about it with my coach. Once it was written up on the whiteboard, it became real. Within a year, I was trained and authorised. I've had a more vibrant life as a result. I've spent many Saturdays at lovely locations officiating at weddings. I've loved working with families for the naming ceremonies of their children. It's been a privilege to officiate at funerals and to contribute to easing the grief of families at those sorrowful times.

A common quote often used is 'A goal that's not written down is only a dream.' I can confirm that for me, that's true. Learn from me. Set goals and write them down! It's not negotiable.

Are you thinking, 'I've tried that. It doesn't work'? Some people would say that there are disadvantages to setting goals. I've heard some people say they believe setting goals can create unnecessary stress and pressure, giving you a sense of failure and distracting you from emerging opportunities. I disagree.

Personal project 4: Use the SMART formula to set goals

Think about a goal that's relevant for you and write it down in the SMART formula:

- What is your specific goal?
- How will you measure its achievement?
- Is it attainable?
- Is it relevant?
- What's the time frame to achieve it?

Put your written goals somewhere where you will see them every day – multiple times is good. I know someone who writes them on the inside of her shower cubicle.

 You can use the editable worksheet on my website. www.everywhensolutions.com.au/resources

You need to be in good shape to kick goals

When you're setting goals, it could be when you're feeling emotionally and physically depleted. If that's stopping you, think about what you need to refuel. Is it food or rest? Is it doing something creative? Go for a walk, get yourself in the headspace to think about the future. Even setting a smaller goal can help.

Many of us read research around resting our brains from social media and devices before we go to sleep. Not all of us act on the research. Here's an example of setting a small goal that might help you get in better shape. How about setting a goal to read a book instead of social media before you sleep tonight?

S – I'm going to read my novel before I go to sleep tonight instead of social media.

M – I'm going to read ten pages.

A – yes, it's attainable.

R – it's relevant; my book is excellent, I love the author, and it's just sitting beside my bed.

T – I'm going to do this tonight.

When you are setting your SMART goals, keep them as simple as possible. Don't overthink the process. Test your thinking with others whom you trust. If you are depleted and thinking that you're not up to the task, fill your fuel tank with whatever it is you need.

Personal Project 4 – SMART goal worksheet. You can find an editable version on my website. www.everywhensolutions.com.au/resources

Planning

Remember that planning is a core component of being in the zone of conscious grit.

Change can be frightening. For some, it might be tempting to ignore your tipping point and continue with your tenacious and determined nose to the grindstone. You are about to do something amazing, but there will be voices in your head questioning what you're doing. There will be practical matters to consider.

The planning I'm talking about is in addition to the setting of the goals using the SMART model. After using that model, you have your goals written down. To achieve your goals, you will need to work out the steps that move you closer.

Here is a simple method using sticky notes and a wall in your home or at work:

- Write the actions that need to happen on sticky notes – one per note.
- Put them on your wall and move them around so that they are in a sequence that makes sense.
- As you notice actions that are missing, add them.
- Cluster the notes in terms of when they need to happen – today, next week, next month, for example.

Now you have a plan. It's simple and effective. It will reduce the risks of you leaving out a specific step or detail. It will also reduce the chance of you forgetting to include someone in the communication process. Your change process can be upset if you tell someone what you are up to and then they tell one of your important people before you do! Something as simple as that can sabotage your grand plan.

Avoid perfectionism. Your planning can be sound, your direction achievable and yet you feel it's not ready to launch, because it's not perfect. If you wait until it's 'perfect', you will never act. Also, we rarely get to 'finish' whatever it is we have planned to do, certainly not in the exact way we envisioned it. I remember at one point in my then emerging executive career, I very nearly declined an opportunity because 'I had unfinished business'! Thankfully a very wise mentor told me there will always be unfinished business. He said it was unrealistic to think that I could wrap up one role with a nice, neat ribbon and move on to the next one. I've needed to remember this many times.

I should have known this, just by living life in general. Have you ever done a home renovation or a room makeover? You have a vision, you set a goal, you plan, and you do the renovations or makeover. It's great and you are happy. Three years later, you are still adding a pot plant here, taking a picture off there, changing the wall colour and adding new cushions. None of that was in your original plan. You could say your plan wasn't perfect. But you got what you wanted at the time.

Mindset

Fixed mindset and growth mindset, as defined by Carol Dweck[8] in her book *Mindset: Changing the Way You Think to Fulfil Your Potential,* will limit or enhance your opportunity to fulfil your potential. She says that it is unlikely that you will see the potential of a tipping point if you are not in a growth mindset.

Dweck says that people with a growth mindset embrace challenges and persist in the face of setbacks. They might feel fear but are happy to give it a go anyway. They see everything they do as an advancement in growing skills and knowledge. They're on the path to mastery but importantly they know they don't have to be masters now. They don't get discouraged if they are not perfect or haven't got there 'yet', but they are driven to keep advancing.

Given a problem, people with a fixed mindset tend to personalise the problem and think, 'I'm just this way, I don't have any ideas about how to sort that out.'

---

8   Dweck, C 2017, *Mindset: Changing the Way You Think to Fulfil Your Potential,* Little, Brown Book Group, United Kingdom

In contrast, people in a growth mindset think, 'This is a hard problem. I haven't been up against this one before. What are my options?'

In a fixed mindset, people ignore useful negative feedback. However, in a growth mindset, they learn from criticism.

In a fixed mindset, they see effort as fruitless. In a growth mindset, they see effort as the path to better things.

Growth mindset is needed every day. When families interact and when human beings work alongside each other, often it's not smooth sailing. We all experience interactions in the family and in the workplace that make us feel uncomfortable. It's easy to think, 'I don't want to deal with that.'

With a growth mindset you think, 'Actually, that's okay. This is just a challenge; we can work that out. Yes, that person is being difficult but let's keep trying to find a way to work together.'

You can move between mindsets

The good news is that you can move from a fixed mindset to a growth mindset. The more we think in growth mindset, the stronger our neural pathways grow in that way. More about that in Chapter Eight.

It would be a shame to reach a tipping point but then be paralysed to move because you have a fixed mindset. That is a life-changing opportunity lost.

Here's a quote from W Timothy Gallwey[9], in his book *The Inner Game of Tennis*. He says:

> *When we plant a rose seed in the earth, we notice that it is small, but we do not criticise it as 'rootless and stemless'. We treat it as a seed, giving it the water and nourishment required of a seed ... Within it, at all times, it contains its whole potential. It seems to be constantly in the process of change; yet at each stage, at each moment, it is perfectly all right as it is.*

A person with a fixed mindset will read this and think:

- it's only a small seed
- it takes a long time to do anything
- it takes lots of water and nourishment
- it's taking a long time to be a rose.

A person with a growth mindset will think:

- amazing to think that tiny seed will grow into a rose
- let's make sure it gets enough water and nourishment for the months that it needs to grow into a rose
- the long wait to see the rose will be worth it.

Meet Gail in growth mindset.

We moved into our new house when the children were very young. We had next to no money, no garden. There was dirt and I wasn't much of a gardener. However, I put in grass and a couple of small garden beds. It was a sign of a growth mindset. I recognised that it was worthwhile and the more gardening I did, the better I got. My growth mindset drove success.

---

9   Gallwey, WT 1979, *The Inner Game of Tennis*, Bantam Books, Toronto

Meet Anneke.

Anneke is a young woman who comes from a low socioeconomic area. When I first got to know her, she was a single mum who had been working part time in administrative roles. Her mindset was, 'I'm a single mum. I've got this kid. That's my lot in life. No point studying.' There was a tipping point for her that came from her own maturation, her observation of people who became her role models and encouragement from others. She resumed her abandoned university study. Her mindset became, 'It would be a real challenge for me to do university study, but if they think I can do it, then I think I can do it. And I'm going to do it.'

Her story demonstrates the significant impact that we have on the mindset of others. This happens in a deliberate way through mentoring. It also happens when role models are observed by others. All of us can help those around us have a growth mindset. When that happens, everyone benefits.

Growth mindset as a problem solver

Growth mindset is about being confident there is a solution. It can be done. Here's an example.

In 2014, I was completing my Master of Public Administration. My dad was in intensive care and in a bad way. My mum had multiple sclerosis and Parkinson's disease. She was in a nursing home and was not able to speak well due to her illnesses. She was also unable to walk. I was involved in a significant project for my study program that required collaboration with others in Victoria, Canberra and New Zealand. Given our workloads during the day, we had phone conferences in the evenings. In the winter, with deadlines looming, it was common for me to do my full-time job, and then drive to the hospital. I would wait for the maxi-taxi that I'd arranged to transport mum in her wheelchair, and then take her out of the maxi-taxi and up to see Dad. I'd spend a few minutes with Dad, get an update on his condition from the medical staff and leave them together. I would sit in my car with the engine running and the heater on – it was mid-winter in Hobart – and dial in to the teleconference.

When that finished around 8 pm, I would go back into the hospital, watch their sad and teary goodbyes and bring Mum down in the lift. We would wait for the maxi-taxi and ensure she had a blanket around her for the trip. I would follow the taxi back to the nursing home and then get her out. Given the lateness of the hour, I'd wheel her through the main building and down through the freezing outdoor parking area to the facility where her room was. I would find staff, let them know she was back, and wait with her 'til someone came to help toilet her – by that time, she needed to go! My mother and I both stretched ourselves. We embraced the challenge. We succeeded in that mission to ensure that she and Dad could see each other during that challenging difficult time. This is an example of a growth mindset – on her part and mine.

Growth mindset at work

I'm sure many of us have been involved in groups where there has been a discussion with lots of opinions being put forward – at work or around the family table. Wherever the discussions are being held, there may be critical or sensitive decisions to be made. Carol Dweck reports research by Robert Wood where two groups were observed undertaking a complex management task. The researchers found that the members of the growth mindset groups were more prone to state their honest opinions and openly express their disagreements. The fixed mindset groups had concern about who was smart or dumb and had anxiety about disapproval for their ideas. Open, productive discussion did not happen.

Here's another example where a growth mindset is needed. You may have experienced those people who cut you off in a meeting. They have a level of knowledge that they think is superior. You don't get the opportunity to contribute as you wish. They are demonstrating a fixed mindset where their own success and talent is their strongest motivation. In growth mindset you take a deep breath, know that you will get some strange looks around the table, prepare your thoughts and embrace the challenge of getting your point across. Good work!

Fixed mindset can have poor consequences

Don't be like Lilli, a repeat drink-driving offender with a fixed mindset.

Lilli drives with alcohol in her system. She knows she exceeds the legal limit. Lilli is pulled over on a Wednesday evening and loses her driver's licence for twelve months. It's not the first time she has been caught. There is no one to blame but herself. She is responsible. Lilli wastes a lot of energy blaming, being angry with the police and making up excuses about why the police shouldn't have pulled her over that evening. Lilli would do much better to learn from the moment. Like some others with a fixed mindset, Lilli has a tendency to blame others. Her mindset is not serving her well. She is not open to learning. After this scenario, Lilli offended on further occasions and was eventually given a custodial sentence.

Some tips to maintain a growth mindset

Maintaining a growth mindset requires effort and we can all do it. Here are some tips:

- Humans are hard-wired for negativity so be conscious of that and replace negative thoughts about yourself or others with compassionate and kind thoughts.
- If you get caught up in negative thinking patterns, replace your thoughts with facts.
- Recognise successes and enjoy them.
- Remember what you are grateful for and why.
- Trust your thoughts about what would make things better.
- Mistakes and failures are learning opportunities.
- Continue to consciously stretch yourself.
- Note when you say 'No' and ask 'Is there a different way?'
- Ask someone to tell you when you are demonstrating fixed mindset characteristics.

Don't be a 'yes' person

I don't want you to get the wrong impression. Having a growth mindset isn't about saying yes to everything. It isn't about believing that every challenge has an immediate solution or that only you can sort it out. Rather, it's about stretching yourself. It is about saying yes to being your authentic self, embracing challenges and persisting during setbacks.

There are some circumstances where it's tempting to be the person who just says 'yes'. Let's say in the workplace, you're in a team meeting. The boss proposes a shift in policy. Everyone is too scared to say no to the boss, so everybody nods, and the policy shift is adopted. The person with the growth mindset will be the one who knows it will be a challenge to push back on the boss but will stretch themselves to put forward an alternative position.

If you have children, then you will know how tempting it is to say yes to every request a child makes. You also know it's not good for them or for you to do that. It's about figuring out what you're going to say yes to and having some boundaries in place. A person with a growth mindset will stretch themselves to find a way to negotiate and find common ground with the children.

Personal project 5: What can you control?

One way to assess if you have a growth mindset is to think about what things you believe you have control over. Give a tick to those things if you believe you have control over them.

	✓
1. Your happiness	
2. What you think about	
3. What you talk about	
4. What you eat	
5. How kind you are	
6. What you believe	
7. Your level of effort	
8. The people you spend time with	
9. When you go to bed	
10. How much you laugh	

If you don't have ten ticks, you might not be in a growth mindset. Read the list again. Remember YOU have control over everything on this list.

You can print this list from www.everywhensolutions.com.au/resources

You might not realise you are in a fixed mindset

You can be in a fixed mindset for parts of your life, and growth mindset for other parts.

At times – and particularly when you are under pressure – you may subtly indicate to others that you are in a fixed mindset. You might not even recognise it. This happened to me.

At one point in my life, a coach noticed how I use the words 'winning', 'battle', 'losing', 'back foot'. I used those words a lot and he was right to point it out to me. I was having a few challenges and I'd resorted to the language that reflected the internal chaos that I was sorting out. For me, it was simple. I was winning or I was losing. But a conscious shift in language on my part was helpful.

It was no coincidence that the matter I was dealing with was resolved when I stopped looking at it as a war event.

I started reframing my thinking and asking my colleagues, 'What options do we have? What are the benefits of doing this? Where are we at with that?'

Here is the visual summary from the previous chapter, with the learnings from this chapter added in. You are now doing even better in the zone of conscious grit. You are not yet unstoppable. But you will be by the end of the book.

CHAPTER FIVE

Be ready. It won't be pretty

The best way to treat obstacles is to use them as stepping-stones. Laugh at them, tread on them, and let them lead you to something better.

— Enid Blyton, *Mr Galliano's Circus*

Prepare for transition

In this chapter, I want to prepare you for what you will face when you enter the transition from one zone to the other. You will come up against obstacles; expect them, accept them and use them to your advantage, just as Enid Blyton suggests in her book *Mr Galliano's Circus*.

Like anything in life, we do better when we've had practice. Moving into a new way of thinking and acting is full of risk. You are bound to make mistakes, get scared and maybe even wish you hadn't found that tipping point.

My inclination was to second-guess myself with thoughts like, 'Oh! I've made a mistake. I've taken a misstep. I'm a bad person. The situation wasn't so bad, after all, and I should have stayed there.' I should've, I could've, I would've.

As with any transition, there is confusion. The confusion does lead to creativity, even though you feel frustrated and disoriented. You start to look at things in a new light. You see new options. These are the makings of new beginnings. You begin to feel optimistic about the future. You get cautiously excited about a new way of being and doing things in a way you hadn't tried or thought possible before.

You will be more visible to those around you. This was problematic for me. When I was doing the best I could and in the zone of unconscious grit, it was easier for those around me. Once I decided to plan for a new future, everyone had a judgement about my situation or an opinion about what I should do. It was tempting to give in to those pressures. And if I had, my plan would have been derailed.

The challenge was to be authentic. At the time, I didn't even know what that meant. I now know that being authentic is crucial to being successful in all areas of life.

In this chapter, I'm going to tell you about the importance of being authentic. I'll give you a tool that you pull out of your toolbox and use for tricky situations, and a framework for making those changes.

Be your authentic self

There is a link between grit and authenticity. Stephen Joseph, in *Authentic: How to Be Yourself and Why It Matters* (see footnote 5), notes that Swedish researchers Vainio and Daukantaite carried out surveys to assess authenticity and grit. They found that those who scored higher on authenticity were more likely to score higher on a measure of grit. He says that authentic people will be more motivated to pursue their goals no matter what it takes.

I believe that to be true.

But what does it mean to be authentic? Joseph says that 'Authentic people have a number of common characteristics that show that they're psychologically mature and fully functioning as human beings.'

He goes on to say that authentic people have realistic perceptions of reality. They're accepting of themselves and other people, they're thoughtful and able to express their emotions freely and clearly, they're open to learning from their mistakes, and they understand their motivations.

When you are committed to living in the zone of conscious grit, you will find it easier to stay there if you are authentic.

Authenticity has a long history as one of the core concepts of humanistic psychology, but the terminology has changed over the years. You might be familiar with Maslow's description of the state of self-actualisation. Self-actualised people are realistic in their perceptions, accept themselves and others, are guided by personal goals and values, form deep relationships, and do not need approval.

Carl Rogers described the state of fully functioning in the 1960s. He said this involved moving away from facades, pleasing others and meeting expectations, and moving towards self-direction, openness to experience, acceptance of others, and trusting one's self.

This quote from Apple CEO, the late Steve Jobs describes the state of being authentic. He says:

> *Your time is limited, so don't waste it living someone else's life. Don't be trapped by dogma, which is living with the results of other people's thinking. Don't let the noise of others' opinions drown out your inner voice, and most important, have the courage to follow your heart and intuition because they somehow already know what you truly wanted to become.*

Know yourself, own yourself and be yourself

Depending on your past experiences, you might think that it's just not possible for you to live an authentic life. Perhaps you have been living a life where you haven't been true to yourself. There is no judgement from me on that one. The important thing is to recognise that you are, or have been, living inauthentically and you want to change that. Stephen Joseph says authenticity demands that we face up to ourselves and tell the truth to ourselves. We need to have full awareness of the consequences of our actions. Sometimes this is not our 'go-to' way of being.

In short, if you give in to external influences dragging you in a direction that is not consistent with your gut feelings, then you are not living with authenticity.

Joseph says there are three things authentic people do: they know themselves, own themselves, and be themselves. What does that mean? Here's a summary based on his thoughts.

People who know themselves do these things	People who don't know themselves do these things
They listen to their inner voice, their gut and their feelings and they hear their inner wisdom.	They get confused about emotions and make poor decisions for themselves, often doing what they think will please others.
They will not let others bully them into taking a position that they disagree with, and they take responsibility for their choices in life.	They don't learn from what has happened, and they blame others.
They work out how to live, consistent with their beliefs and motivations. They say what they mean and mean what they say.	They live in ways where what they say and do don't match how they think and feel.

Authenticity in action

In moving into the zone of conscious grit, I was starting to flex my authentic-self muscles. I didn't know that at the time. My story continues with the sale of the home that we'd bought and enjoyed together before Peter became ill. Furniture, money, and other possessions were divided. My parents had a house with a rumpus room downstairs, so the children and I moved there. Jason loved being there. He and my mum had always had a special relationship. Maybe that's because she was present at his birth. Alanna was about 8 months old and was a terrible sleeper, so I spent hours walking the hilly streets with her in the pram, going home when she'd fallen asleep. Staying with Mum and Dad was not a long-term proposition from my perspective. There was no pressure from them to move out, but I had developed a strong drive to get on with things. I was impatient to lay down the foundations of our new life.

We needed some independent housing. Renting in the private market was going to be out of my reach, and I was horrified that I would have to use public housing. I didn't want to live in the broadacre areas that were a feature of public housing. Then I discovered a new, small public housing subdivision being developed about ten minutes' drive from Mum and Dad's place. When I drove around, there were a few homes almost finished and several allotments that were yet to be built on. I decided that I wanted one of those. This was a determined, tenacious, future-focused gritty aim.

Fortunately for us, this was when government systems were more personal and easier to navigate. There was no such thing as applying online. You either spoke to someone on the phone or met with them in person. I used my 'big C' Courage, made an appointment with the manager and pleaded my case, with both children in tow. Jason missed a morning of school, but I thought it was worth it to make my case as real as possible.

We moved into the house on what was still a subdivision and a building site. There were no fences and no garden. But it was a sign that our life was coming together. It was close enough for Peter to visit and then walk home, or for his mother to pick him up. Sometimes Jason would go to Peter's home for a visit.

In taking this action, I now know I acted with authenticity. I accepted responsibility for my housing situation. I was true to myself in that I didn't want to rely on my family. I was realistic about what we could afford, and I understood my motivation. I continued to press ahead to create a safer life for us, despite others not being able to accept my motivation or decisions. I was open to creating a life that was different and I trusted myself and my judgements.

Personal project 6: Check in to the manifesto for authentic living

In his book, *Authentic: How to Be Yourself and Why It Matters*, Stephen Joseph has a manifesto for authentic living. It includes five points on how to take authenticity forward in your life:

- Know your boundaries and be clear to others about what is acceptable to you and what isn't.
- Use every challenge in life as an opportunity to learn about yourself.
- Be aware of how you feel in the moment and question why those feelings have come about.
- Listen to your gut reactions and what they are telling you, and distinguish your inner voice of wisdom.
- Accept yourself as you are.

On a scale of 1–5, with 5 being more authentic, where do you put yourself for each of them? What will you do to move closer to a 5 (or to stay there, if you're already there!)?

 You can find an editable version of this personal project at www.everywhensolutions.com.au/resources

The Cloak of Uninsultability

The Cloak of Uninsultability – the Cloak – is a tool that you can use when you are under fire or when you think that you are going to be under fire. I was introduced to this concept by Mary Dwyer (see www.MaryCDwyer.com) from Impact Solutions International at what was for me a life-changing leadership course.

We all need a trick or two

Uninsultability isn't a real word. A Cloak of Uninsultability isn't a real thing. But the term says what it means. It's imaginary, and you visualise putting it on when you feel you will be under pressure, in conflict or criticised. You put it on when you feel vulnerable, and you know that it will help you through that moment.

It's hard work being consistently tenacious, persistent, resilient, determined, and future-focused! Everyone needs a trick or two to call on when required, and this is one of them. It's not a tool you use all the time. It's for when you need it.

I didn't know about the imaginary but effective Cloak of Uninsultability when I needed it. I just dealt with criticism, judgement, and negative opinions. I didn't deal with them well. Some of it hurt. A lot. Some of it stuck. For a long time.

A cloak for special occasions

Several years ago, the executive team I was in adopted this tool, and it became part of our culture. Let me give you an example of how this was helpful. Over several months, I was one of a few people targeted in a cyber-bullying event. A person had set up an email address under a fake name and fabricated stories about four executives, including me. They repeatedly emailed media outlets, the premier and other ministers with mischievous fabrications. The media printed some of them. It was a challenging time, and it went on for months. Experts in cyber-security were not able to trace the source.

One day another email arrived in the inbox of the CEO. He told me that I was not to worry about it. He later rang me and said, 'Gail, I think you need to put your Cloak on. It's not as innocuous as I first thought.' This technique had given us a practical and useful tool, and a universal language that we could use to support each other.

The Cloak helped me rationalise the experience and let it sit on the outside of my Cloak which was black, impenetrable, and worn with stilettos.

My colleague and friend Kim's Cloak was made of gossamer. She says it was like fairy wings – it wrapped around her, and she would levitate, the insults and issues swirling around her but not touching her. She was able to look at situations objectively and identify problems without feeling personally involved. Kim still uses this tool many years later. She recently found herself the target of frustration from people who were tasked with working together to find a solution to a community issue. She used her beautiful gossamer Cloak to deflect the criticism – which wasn't about her but the processes of other organisations. She was able to stay focused on the issues and to get the outcomes required.

My friend and colleague Annie also designed her Cloak years ago. Hers was royal blue velvet with a lead lining to prevent any barbs from getting through. Annie used her Cloak many times when she delivered challenging or difficult news to the team she was managing. As time went on, she realised that the Cloak was a tool she could use to ensure her emotions were not being overwhelmed by the feelings of those around her.

Recently, Annie officiated as the celebrant at her brother's funeral service attended by nearly 300 people. She put on her Cloak and breathed deeply. As a result, she delivered an exceptionally long service and stood just outside the depth of emotion in the room. She was able to stay out of the emotional pool, speak powerfully, and keep it together through the twelve minutes of montage – the part of funeral services that usually causes the most stoic person to crumble. This was a real test of the Cloak's efficacy. Afterward, in her own time, she took off the Cloak and let the tears flow, proud that she had fulfilled the role. Her late brother had told her, 'No wobbly voices,' and there were none, thanks to the Cloak.

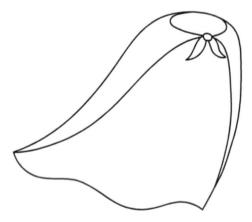

This is a tool for a moment in time

The physiology of the brain drives your reaction to criticism and negative feedback. Your amygdala and prefrontal cortex are activated in these times. When you use the Cloak, you are not trying to stop those natural reactions. It isn't healthy to have the Cloak in place all the time. We all need to experience discomfort to learn and grow. But sometimes you just need a trick that will help you get through the moment or the day. And the Cloak may just be the tool you need.

Personal project 7: Design your Cloak

Take five minutes to visualise what your Cloak might be. What material is it made from? What colour is it? How does it feel? Is it heavy on you? Think about where you're going to keep it – where you can get to it quickly. Scribble down a drawing or description and pop it somewhere safe.

If you don't feel that you can be creative, choose a Cloak that's already been invented. Any number of superheroes have capes or cloaks – Superman, Batman, Thor, Captain Marvel, Wonder Woman. Even Fred Flintstone's animal print suit will do – even though it's not a cape. It's the concept that's important. And remember it's a temporary little trick you can use. The aim is not to dull your ability to soak up feedback, learn, and grow.

Visualise your Cloak in your toolbox and know it's there anytime you need it.

I'd love to see what you come up with. Draw your cloak or describe it in a word picture and email to me at gail@everywhensolutions.com.au

Changemaker framework

When you decide to deal with any adverse situation and enter the conscious grit zone, you are in the process of change. Using a model to guide you will give you the best chance of success in moving through the process.

This is different to having a plan. In the context of this book, having a plan is the 'what' you will do to get where you need to go. The plan sits within the changemaker framework.

In my executive and leadership roles over thirty-odd years, I've instigated, led, loved, and been frustrated by many change processes. Those that I've been frustrated by are those that do not have a framework around them. Without a framework, the idiosyncrasies of human behaviour can disrupt the change process, setting it back in terms of timing, or derailing it completely.

There are many models for implementing change. One that you might be familiar with is Lewin's[10] 1940s model of unfreeze, change, and refreeze. Lewin is a physicist as well as a social scientist. He uses the concept of shifting a cube of ice to become a cone of ice. First, you need to unfreeze the cube, pour the water into the cone shape, and then refreeze it.

In other words, you need to find the motivation to change – to unfreeze. Then you make the change to the new way of being and refreeze in the new state. For example, if you are motivated to lose 10 kg for health reasons, you could go to the dietician and get a plan. Then you start the program (unfreezing your prior eating habits) and stick with it for thirty days (making the change), after which the new diet's pattern is embedded (refreezing into the new way of diet and exercise).

Thought leader and management consultant Professor John Kotter[11] developed another model. I've used his eight-step process countless times in the workplace. You can find it in full here: https://

---

10   https://en.wikipedia.org/wiki/Kurt_Lewin
11   https://en.wikipedia.org/wiki/John_Kotter

www.kotterinc.com/wp-content/uploads/2019/04/8-Steps-eBook-Kotter-2018.pdf

I've been inspired by Kotter's model to develop a framework for you to use when you want to be a changemaker in your own life.

	Changemaker Framework
Step One	Acknowledge that you are stuck and are in the zone of unconscious grit. Know that you are tenacious, determined, resilient, persistent and using 'little c' courage; these are all positive traits. Find and catch a tipping point (see Chapter Three). Move into in the zone of conscious grit. Put on your Cloak.
Step Two	Appoint your 'kitchen cabinet' – the small group to be your supporters and the people you go to for a reality check when you need it; the people you trust implicitly.
Step Three	Set SMART goals (see Chapter Four) and commit to some deliberate planning about what you will do and when.
Step Four	Identify who you need in your network for practical support. Get your growth mindset happening and commit to maintaining it throughout.
Step Five	Realise that life is a dance. You will learn lots of new dances. Some will be harder than others. Commonly they will involve steps forward, back, sideways, with some random twirling and a possible loss of balance.
Step Six	Recognise progress, celebrate and value the contributions of others.
Steps Seven and onwards	Repeat. Persist. Tweak. Repeat. Persist. Tweak. Repeat.

You can use this framework in many situations.

Here's a scenario that shows how it fits together.

Meet Nicole.

Nicole has been trying hard to make ends meet. The bills don't stop. There are all sorts of demands on her budget. She has been tenacious, determined and persistent in reducing expenditure. Nicole has maxed out her credit cards and is unable to make the multiple monthly payments. Reality sets in. That's the tipping point.

Nicole moves into the zone of conscious grit. She adds a future focus and a plan to the way she has been approaching the problem while in the zone of unconscious grit.

Nicole develops a budget and decides she will put her Cloak on every time the kids ask her for things that she can't afford. She appoints her mum to her kitchen cabinet and tells her the situation. Nicole feels much better now she has shared the load, and her mum offers to cut up her credit cards for her. Nicole agrees. Nicole decides that she wants to have a holiday in twelve months and to have paid off her credit card debt.

She sets a SMART goal.

S – the credit card debt will be paid off within eight months and in twelve months, she and the kids will have a week by the beach as a reward.

M – it's measurable, with the zero debt and time frames allocated.

A – it's attainable. Nicole is promoted for the next eighteen months into a higher-level role with increased salary.

R – it's relevant. She doesn't want to have the debt.

T – the time is right to do this, and the time allocated to achieve the goal is doable.

Nicole talks to the children and tells them the problem, the goals and how they can contribute.

Nicole has embraced the challenge. She has a plan. She is bouncing back. She has a growth mindset. She didn't quite make the holiday in twelve months, but at fourteen months she booked it and they went on their holiday three months after that.

Tips when using the changemaker framework

- The tipping point will be there somewhere. Be vigilant and catch it when you find it.

- Choose trusted friends and family for your kitchen cabinet. Keep it a small group.

- Think about what qualities you'd want in the people in your kitchen cabinet across the group. It's essential to have the following qualities collectively: people who are patient, have enough experience to be wise, who are a little conservative, not easily flustered, respected by many, smart, practical, action-oriented, not intimidated, trusted, curious, creative, level-headed, logical. A sense of humour is also important.

- Some people might need to be convinced that they should be in your kitchen cabinet. You might have to explain that there's something in it for them; that the problem affects them, directly or indirectly. With me, it was easy. My parents wanted me and the children to be safe. I think they also thought that if they could help me get sorted out, then their life as they envisioned it might be returned to them!

- If someone doesn't want to be in your kitchen cabinet, don't pressure them into it. If you value their input – just ask if you can have an occasional catch-up with them as a sounding board.

- Be aware that some others may not see your issues in the same way that you do. They may not have your best interests at heart. Be careful about who you engage with. Keep looking until you find the person who can help. It's the same as finding a new hairdresser because yours has retired. You need to find the one you connect with and trust.

- Stay determined even if you get a bit wobbly in the dance.

- Others may not recognise progress, but if you do, celebrate it.

I present this framework as if it's linear. It's not. It's life after all and we have to expect the unexpected. One of the features of this model is that it's okay to jump a step forward or go back a couple of steps. You use it as a guide and make sure that all the components are covered. I have laid it out in such a way that makes linear sense, and if it works for a particular situation in that way, that's okay. But often you will need to move around. One of the frequent changes to the order is that you might want to get your kitchen cabinet together before you take action. Often you will know that certain people will be able to help you. They may even be the people who will help you find your tipping point into the conscious grit zone. You can use the changemaker framework in a flexible way.

Download the framework from www.everywhensolutions.com.au/resources

Personal project 8: Be a changemaker

So, you have decided that a change is needed. Map out your thinking below as you reflect on these questions.

- What do you want to change?
- What was your tipping point?
- Are you using all the capabilities of being in the zone of conscious grit?
- What does your Cloak of Uninsultability look like?
- Who is in your kitchen cabinet?
- Have you written your goals in the SMART format?
- What skills do you have in your broader network?
- Are you missing any?
- Are you ready to dance?
- How are you going to recognise progress and celebrate?
- Are you committed to continually tweak your process and stay the course?

You now know that when you are doing big things, at times it's not pretty. Sometimes the reactions of others may be so extreme when you are managing difficult situations that you shift from being wobbly to being entirely off-balance. Being your authentic self will keep you on balance (most of the time). Your Cloak will help you to not go off balance. The Changemaker Model will be your guide and a reliable framework so that you don't tackle the tough stuff alone.

 These tools are the additional components you use when you are in the zone of conscious grit.

Nearly unstoppable

The diagram shows that you have been gathering skills since you reached the stage of being unstuck. You are nearly unstoppable!

CHAPTER SIX

You don't know what you don't know

As you get older and you realise you really don't know as much as you think you know, you listen more. Because then you think, now I need to be more receptive to the things I don't know. That's how you learn.

— Phil Keoghan, Host of *The Amazing Race*

Other people can be a help or a hindrance!

In this chapter, I give you lots of information that I wish I'd known those years ago. It's information that will help you understand how you and others perform as human beings. In short, the chapter speaks to a short statement: other people can be both a help and a hindrance!

You will read some personal anecdotes from me about how some of my childhood experiences have shown up in my adult years as limiting beliefs. I want to make it clear that my parents did their best as parents, just as I have done as a parent. You and yours would have done the same. Some may feel that I am critical of them as parents – I am not. They brought to their parenting their background, circumstances, their limiting beliefs and their own understanding of the times in which they were living. We all do this. While my lovely mum and dad are mentioned in some of my stories, my childhood was a happy one where I knew I was loved and cared for by two incredibly good people. I miss them a lot.

I've discovered that life is upside down. The longer you live, the more you know. However, often in your younger years, you need to know what you now know. When I look back at managing the time after Peter's illness, I realise I was missing lots of knowledge. I was also missing the ability to find what might be helpful for me. I was on automatic pilot. I had no framework or structure to understand how humans work when under significant pressure. I was doing the best I could to find a way to respond to day-to-day life but could not think about or plan for the future. I was feeling flattened and isolated. I didn't know my limiting beliefs were impacting and crushing any initiative that I may have had. I didn't know what I didn't know.

There is information everywhere. Sometimes it falls in your lap. Often you need to find it. To see it, you need to know where to look and have ideas about what to look for. If we don't look up and out, the risk is that we get stuck because we don't know what we don't know. We disadvantage ourselves because we don't have the information to make good choices and sound judgements.

After Peter became unwell, I muddled around (albeit determined, persistent and tenacious) because I didn't know what I didn't know. I didn't even know where to get information to help me deal with and improve my situation. Often, we don't get a chance to practise our responses. I had never been a young woman with a baby before. Let alone with a baby and a husband with an acquired brain injury who had specific care needs. In fairness, neither those closest to me nor Peter had experience in that either. If we were able to practise our responses to situations, we would know a bit more. But again, we don't know what we don't know because we don't get to practise and figure out the gaps.

It's like when you do first-aid training and for the first six months are confident that if you needed to apply CPR, you could do it well. But you don't need to use that skill for the next two years. When someone has collapsed in front of you, you don't know what you don't know. You don't know what's changed in the past two years. So, your confidence drops. You do it the best you can. But you may have done a better job if you did know what you didn't know.

Hard-wiring

Nigel Nicholson[12] says that *Homo sapiens* emerged on the Savannah Plain some 200,000 years ago, yet according to evolutionary psychology, people today still seek those traits that made survival possible then. This includes the instincts to fight when threatened, and to trade information and share secrets. He says you can take the person out of the Stone Age, but you can't take the Stone Age out of the person.

His thoughts are reinforced by the work of primatologist Dr Jane Goodall.[13] She states that chimpanzees and human beings have

---

12   Nicholson, N 1998, 'How hardwired is human behavior?', *Harvard Business Review*, vol. 76, no. 4, p. 134. Accessed 22 November 2020, at https://hbr.org/1998/07/how-hardwired-is-human-behavior

13   https://janegoodall.ca/our-work/research/all-about-chimps/

only a 1% difference in DNA. The community and social structures of chimpanzees are remarkably similar to humans, and the behaviours that we see in chimpanzees are hard-wired, much like those in humans. Observing the functioning of the chimpanzees gives us an insight into the hard-wired behaviours of humans. Dr Goodall says that we can analyse the traits that we share with chimpanzees and use that to understand why we behave the way we do. When we understand the complex ways chimpanzees maintain social harmony in their communities, we find insights for dealing with tensions between individuals and groups of humans.

This has become obvious to me over my years in both executive management and life in general. I attended a course on-site at Taronga Zoo in 2018, run by Andrew O'Keeffe[14], the author of *Hardwired Humans*, and observed the chimps there, to progress my understanding of how human beings are hard-wired.

In his book, Andrew O'Keeffe describes nine human instincts. The first is that humans desire a sense of belonging. The second is that social groups function through a hierarchy. The other seven relate to how humans think and feel. Some are obvious when you know the signs.

1. Did you know we put emotion before reasoning? We screen information first using emotion. We screen how something or someone makes us feel, and then we screen for logic. There is a physiological reason for this. Messages are first received by the amygdala, which is the emotional processing part of the brain. The neocortex part of the brain then receives the signals for rational processing. That is why, in the workplace, it is common that even the most

---

14   O'Keeffe, A 2011, *Hardwired Humans: Successful Leadership Using Human Instincts*, Roundtable Press, NSW, Australia

sensible employees have trouble receiving constructive feedback well. Because of the primacy of emotions, people hear the bad news first and loudest. As a manager, I know that where you give positive and negative feedback, it is always the negative feedback that the person hears first and loudest, reacts to and remembers most vividly.

Consider this scenario – it's one that's been repeated several times across my career.

I provide feedback to an individual as part of an annual process. It's a mixture of eight areas where performance has been glowing and two areas where the need for minor improvement was discussed. Improvement suggestions are not significant, and it's certainly not about 'poor performance'. The meeting ends. Inevitably there will be an email that evening, or an appointment pop up in the diary with the request, 'Can we talk more about the areas I need to improve.' Rarely does the employee reflect that the meeting overall was positive. The perceived negative feedback prevailed. You may have been the giver or the receiver in a similar situation.

2. We use our first impressions to classify. Think about this.

    You are walking along a beach, and you hear a loud and aggressive noise coming from an animal that you can't see. It seems to be in the scrub where the beach meets the dunes. Your instinct, using first impressions to classify, tells you that it's a big and savage dog. It might run after you and bite you. You don't want to look. You want to get out of the area as fast as you can.

    However, you challenge your instincts and have a look. In this hypothetical, the dog is caught by its leg in a rabbit trap. The first impression was inaccurate. Our instinct is to think about things as good/bad or fun/boring, or she likes me/she doesn't like me. In this case, the dog was little (not big), was in pain (not savage). Once someone has made their instant assessment, they are unlikely to change their opinion.

3. Humans are more motivated by the avoidance of loss than the opportunity to gain. We believe that when we put something in, we should get something out. So we keep trying to get something back, even when it's lost. Think about the people who have a habit of putting money into poker machines. They want to say that on that day they had a win. But overall, they have lost.

4. While the word 'gossip' has a negative connotation, gossip served our ancestors well. Through the ages, survivors were savvy enough to anticipate power shifts, manipulate others, and adjust for the circumstances. They were skilled at and engaged in gossip. We see it in the workplace. There are always the expert gossipers who know essential information before everyone else does, they chat with just the right people at just the right time and get themselves into a position of advantage. Gossip is useful in the workplace. It helps to get information circulated as well as construct and maintain social alliances. Humans structure themselves to be most effective in their gossip endeavours. Have you ever been chatting to others at a cocktail party, and a fifth person joins a group of four? The group of five will quickly split into a group of two and a group of three. That is, they are driven by the human instinct to have the best gossip session. Although we might think someone is avoiding us, it's not so. It's a human instinct.

I find the hard-wired instinct of gossip fascinating. When I think about the time of Peter's illness and the months and years after, I now realise I was isolated. I inadvertently made that happen. I had my hands full. I didn't have time for close friends or regular catch-ups. I didn't experience the benefits of gossip. I missed out on the benefits of exchanging information and testing ideas.

5. Have you ever said to someone 'You are reading my mind'? Empathy and mind-reading are human instincts. They are the building blocks of gossip. I know I have noticed people who seem skilled at hearing secrets, finding out information, asking probing questions, and engaging in leading conversation. They seem to be able to guess what others are thinking. They are experts at detecting how others are thinking and feeling, by what's written on their faces.

6. We have an instinct to put confidence before realism. Humans are hard-wired to deny reality. We emphasise what is possible, and we underestimate what is practical. An example is my unrealistic, optimistic, I-can-fix-this approach to managing life after Peter's illness. That showed up for me as 'I'll just keep trying, it will be okay' self-talk. But the reality was that it was never going to be okay. How often have you seen change processes in the workplace fail? Often the failure is because the amount of effort needed to implement change is underestimated. Instead, there is a 'come on, we can do it attitude'. There is an underestimation of the effort, resources, time, and capability of people required.

You might relate to this scenario. It's like putting together flat-pack furniture without looking at the instructions. It won't go together, and finally, when it's late on a Saturday afternoon, and you're onto your third beer (or a Tasmanian Sauvignon Blanc in my case), you decide you'll read the instructions. That information was there all the time. It was the piece of information you needed to be able to put your piece of furniture together. But you wasted hours, putting confidence before reality.

7. The last instinct relates to thinking and feeling and is about contest and display. Humans spend time, money, effort and energy making themselves look good. Have you noticed that the more senior staff get better offices and CEOs get the corner offices? The higher salaried staff get the parking spots — but they may not often be in the building to use them. This makes little sense to those in the office all day and who can see the practicalities of freeing up the parking spaces and thinking more creatively about the allocation of office space.

When we understand human instincts and everyday human behaviour, some of the things that we see and feel when interacting with others in our personal and professional lives become clearer. When you understand why humans behave in the way they do, you will be less offended by behaviours and responses to your interactions. You can also plan your interactions and responses to get the best results possible.

Fortunately, I knew about behaviour driven by human instincts some years ago when I encountered a keen 'contest and display' example.

I was a senior female executive having my first encounter with a much older male whom I knew had little regard for females in such lofty positions. The meeting was to discuss safety. He already had my attention: I am conscious of safety, and I wanted to hear what he had to say. His first tactic was to shut the door of the small meeting room. The door did not need to be closed. The second tactic was to place a coloured photo, A4 size, on the table between us. The photo was graphic. It was of an arm and barely connected hand injured by a chainsaw. He didn't need to do that. It wasn't the time for contest and display.

When dealing with challenge or trying to sort out whatever it is you are going through, it's helpful for you to understand your behaviour and motivations. There will be a lot of different reactions, and you will be reading body language and listening to opinions and views. It's helpful to understand them through the filter of hard-wired human instincts.

You might not believe in hard-wiring. You might think that individuals behave in particular ways because they're either good or bad. Indeed, hard-wiring isn't the sole influence on how we behave. Our behaviour is influenced by our circumstances, our personality, our intelligence, and our learned behaviour. But, at our core, there are hard-wired instincts.

In your interactions with others remember that:

- emotions will be triggered – yours and others. Be prepared
- others around you will go to emotion first, rather than hear practicalities or logic
- the first seven words you use for difficult conversations will set the impression you want to make
- it's smart to be upfront if there is any loss involved
- it's helpful to do the tricky communication face to face

- you have the right to act on whatever is the right decision for you; don't be put off course by trying to please others
- you need to communicate with those who do need to know; don't leave people out
- some individuals have more influence and status. Pay attention to them.

Event plus response equals outcome

There is a simple equation. E + R = O. That is, an event plus a response equals an outcome. If you don't like the outcome, don't blame the event. The compelling part of the equation is the response. It's up to you to determine the response. It might not feel like it some days, but you do have so much power!

Events happen all day, every day

All events have a response, and there will always be an outcome. As Jack Canfield says in his book *The Success Principles*[15], every-one has control over three things: their thoughts, the images that they visualise, and their actions. They are all forms of response.

You might want to consider the concepts of unconscious grit and conscious grit as options when choosing a response. While dealing with the aftermath of Peter's illness, I was determined to be a good mum and a good wife. That was my response. I was persistent, tenacious, determined, resilient and used 'little c' courage in that period. Nearly five years is a long time, and there were plenty of challenges along the way. I can see now that I was in the zone of unconscious grit, and that was my overall response

---

15 See www.jackcanfield.com

to the situation. At the time, I thought there was only one way to respond: just keep going!

It reminds me of the film *Sliding Doors*. When I went through the door marked 'zone of unconscious grit', I set off on a path of living my life in a way that wasn't going to be best for any of the people I loved. I was making day-to-day choices that weren't all bad. We had food, housing, a much-loved son, and a series of dogs, a lamb, and a couple of rabbits. And then another baby on the way. But safety was an issue. And there was no plan to address this serious aspect of our lives. There was a point when I walked through the door marked 'zone of conscious grit'. I could feel the difference. My choice was to go in that direction. My response was different.

Meet Jess.

Jess stayed with one employer for many years. She carried out her role to a high standard, was a team player, and was committed to the organisation. She often stepped into more senior-level roles for short-term contracts, but there was always some organisational reason, like the budget or timing, for why she was never appointed permanently. The organisation was often transitioning in and out of reforms. Jess needed financial security.

She could have continued to apply for temporary roles at higher levels and not have financial security. Still, Jess did her homework and discovered that funding for the organisation was subject to some external influences that were well beyond her control. Her response to managing and achieving her financial security, which was the outcome that she wanted, was to apply for roles outside of the organisation. Jess secured a permanent, higher-level position for around $40,000 a year more. She got her desired outcome: financial security.

Our feelings are not our response

It's easy to think that our feelings are a response. In his book *The Success Principles*, author Jack Canfield is clear that they are not. He says that 99% of feelings are an outcome of how you think about something. For example, to feel angry, you first need to think a thought. It may be something like 'There he goes again; he can't ever get it right; he's always wasting money.' And then you get angry.

So, when you treat a feeling as a response to the equation E + R = O, you won't get an outcome you want. Let's say the event is that your partner forgets your anniversary. Your response might be to get angry based on your feelings of 'They don't love me; I don't mean anything to him/her'. The outcome might be some kind of argument, maybe some tears, sulking, and a period of not speaking to each other. If the thought is replaced with 'That's unusual, he/she must have had a busy day', instead of being angry, you become curious. With a different response, there will be a different outcome. For example, you could just say, 'It's our anniversary. I remembered. Did you?' The outcome will be different. Even if they had forgotten, you have created the opportunity for a civil discussion based on curiosity.

Sometimes when you respond, you don't get the outcome that you want straight away for a range of reasons. Your response could be a series of actions that occur over time. You might need to tweak your response or change the timing. It's important to realise that others will have views and opinions. You might start to surprise people with the way you manage your responses. You might get criticised by others. If that's the case, stay strong.

Developing a response needs to be a considered process. You need to stay away from responses that are underpinned by blaming. If you hear yourself saying, 'It's not my fault, it's because of her, the team is responsible for that mess, they always misunderstand me,' you are in a state of blame. If this is the case, your response will be skewed. It won't benefit you. Think about the differences in the scenario below.

'My partner doesn't support my decision to leave work and go to university and finish my qualification. He/she is not ambitious at all. It's all his/her fault.' You may let the opportunity go and then be sullen, silent, withdrawn, negatively talking about them with friends.

Compare with this reframe: 'I let that opportunity go, but that was my decision, and I've realised now that I should have made a different decision. I will contact the university and see if there is any chance I can revisit my enrolment.'

You may need to continue to change responses until you get the outcomes you want. Somebody might say to you, 'You've failed because you tried that, and it didn't work.' But that's not a failure. If you've got your eye on an outcome, you can continue to work towards it. Remember that consciously changing your responses to get where you need to go is positive, constructive, and courageous.

Cognitive biases

We all hold cognitive biases. Here are some examples.

- If you only know a little about something, you might think that's all there is to it and deal with it in a simple way. Here's a scenario to demonstrate this point. Four friends decide to have a weekend away. They leave it to you to choose and book the accommodation. You read reviews about the venue, and you think it sounds exactly right. You book, turn up and then realise that there is no food and beverage service, and the nearest town is 50 km away. Your bias was to deal with your weekend away without too much thought. You had read some great reviews and made your decision on a little bit of information. When you reread the reviews, you realise that the comments were about the scenery, the wildlife, the comfy bed, and the peacefulness. There were no comments about the food and beverage service – because there wasn't any.

- Have you ever been unwell and are convinced you have a horrible disease because that's what your mum had? You do a Google search and get 'facts'. As a result, you're convinced that you are seriously ill. When you eventually go to the doctor, you find that it's a different diagnosis – and nothing at all to be worried about. That's confirmation bias.

- Hindsight bias happens when you unfairly assume that others have the same knowledge. For example, you've been part of a conversation about some new research that your organisation will be using. You start to incorporate that thinking into your day-to-day work. Your colleagues have no idea why you are going down that track. Tension rises. You can't understand why they are not doing the same thing. They can't understand why you are doing what you are doing.

- I'm sure that we have all experienced optimism or pessimism bias. Our mood and emotional state can cause irrational decision-making. Have you ever felt down for no real reason on a Saturday afternoon and gone to have a wander around the shops? You come home when the shops have closed, loaded up with purchases that made you feel better for a moment. But you didn't need them. And you couldn't afford them, but you have them!

- Be aware of a particular cognitive bias called the Barnum or Forer Effect. This is where an individual believes in generalised statements often because of a combination of wishful thinking and hopelessness. We've all been there! Let's say you are on the cusp of making a life-changing decision or taking significant action. But you are feeling wobbly. It's a big deal. Then you wake up on the day of change and read, 'Good news could come your way. Don't rush things. Give Lady Luck the chance to find you.' For some people in tough situations, that could be enough to derail the plan that they do need to put into place.

- In Tasmania, we have an imaginary line in the south of the state. There is a road called Creek Road. If you live south of that, colloquially, you are considered to be living in a more affluent suburb. If you live north of Creek Road, you are on the 'wrong side'. Someone has come up with a term to describe this imaginary line: the flannelette curtain.

I was born and bred on the 'wrong side' of the flannelette curtain. Years ago, in my mid-career, I talked to my boss and told him we had bought a new house. He (from south of the flannelette curtain) said, 'Gail, I hope you are moving south of the flannelette curtain. It will be better for your career.' I wasn't. And I still haven't.

This is an example of implicit bias.

Personal project 9: Reframe your response

Consider these scenarios:

Event: John applies for two jobs in the last six months and doesn't make it to the interview stage.

John thinks: 'I am angry and disappointed.'

Outcome: John is still in the same role five years on and has missed lots of opportunities.

Now, look at how I've reframed it.

Event: John has applied for two jobs in the last six months and doesn't make it to the interview stage.

John responds: 'I'm going to get some advice on preparing a resume and addressing selection criteria. I'm curious as to how I can do better next time.'

Outcome: The next time John applies for a role, he gets to the interview stage.

Initially John's feelings of anger and disappointment were his response. It didn't get him anywhere.

Remember that you will likely have a 'feeling' or an 'emotion'. Be careful not to make that feeling your response.

I've developed a simple model to remind you. Practise using my **Reframe Your Response Sheet**.

First, identify what you want to respond to differently. Your weight? Your relationship? Your career? What else?

I am going to focus on _____ (the event).

I want _____ to be the outcome.

I am feeling _____.

I acknowledge that these feelings are not my response.

My response is going to be _____.

An editable template can be found at
www.everywhensolutions.com.au/resources

Intuition, emotions and responses — it's complicated

If you are depressed or feeling weighed down by responsibilities and worries, your response may be more passive, more short term, and probably won't make any substantial impact. It may not even be based on sound judgement and might be executed at the wrong time. As a result, you might feel deflated and want to give up. Don't give up. Get back to basics and identify if your response is your emotion. If so, figure out the thought that sits behind that emotion. Focus your energy on changing that thought.

Fear may be driving procrastination, and that is stopping you from choosing the best response. Remember that fear is an emotion. Fear is not your response, however tempting it might be to use it as an excuse. You will remember from my story that fear was my response for a long time. But then I didn't know what I didn't know! And now I know, and I'm telling you that fear does not need to be your response. But it's not easy. You might need to get some external support to help you respond. That could be a friend, a counsellor, or a trusted colleague, peer, or mentor.

Don't ignore the power of intuition – the ability to know something in the absence of conscious reasoning. Sometimes that intuition points us to an instinctive reaction, and at other times it leads us to the need for more deliberation. I'm sure you've experienced times when there are things that just feel right and don't feel right.

I am a believer in intuition, and I've used gut feel often in my career journey. More than once, I've 'felt' that the best thing to do was to go backwards to go forward. That's always worked out well for me. One time, my gut told me to apply for a much higher level role. All the odds were against me in terms of experience. I pressed on and was appointed to the position and held it for many years.

Conversely, when I haven't listened to intuition and gut feel, I've paid the price. I made an extremely poor appointment once. My gut told me not to employ this person, and I ignored it. The appointment did not work out, and many of us spent much time and energy ending that employment relationship.

The topic of intuition is subjective, and I've learned that bosses who don't believe in intuition don't respond well to advice 'based on my gut feeling'.

Sometimes decision-making and judgements are not as sound when we are under pressure and feeling stressed. These simple rules can help you choose a response:

- If you are basing your response on a feeling, stop. Right now. Identify the thought that is behind the feeling. Respond to the thought, not the feeling.
- Understand that no one else can choose your response for you.

- Be aware that cognitive bias and hard-wiring are going to influence your choice of response.
- Think about what's working and do more of it.
- Then think about what you were doing that's not working and do less of it.
- What are you not doing that you need to try?

Limiting beliefs

Limiting beliefs are false beliefs that we hold about ourselves. They hold us back. We need to figure out what they are and deal with them.

The kind of limiting beliefs I'm talking about form in childhood as a result of family relationships, interactions, modelling and parenting styles. They often surface in adulthood and can present in many ways, including shame, guilt, lack of self-compassion, or self-doubt. Limiting beliefs are beliefs that hold us back from doing something that we're perfectly capable of doing. You know, those beliefs about us like 'I'm not good enough, my words are boring.' These beliefs can get in the way. I now know that my limiting beliefs contributed to the way I responded and coped with Peter's illness. My limiting beliefs held me in the zone of unconscious grit. According to Jack Canfield, limiting beliefs are universal. We are trained overtly and covertly by the media, our parents, schools, and culture to have those beliefs. But we all deserve to reach our best potential. When we know our limiting beliefs, we can create opposite ones and embed them into our ideas.

Be careful how you name your child

Perhaps odd names can create limiting beliefs. We see unusual baby names from time to time and probably wonder why a parent would lumber their child with such a name. I read that a judge in France intervened to change a girl's name from Nutella to Ella, and told other parents they could not name their son Mini Cooper. In New Zealand, parents were banned from calling their twins Fish and Chips. In Mexico, Robocop has been banned as a name.

I give you this anecdote both in jest and seriousness. I am so pleased that in my childhood years technology wasn't what it is today. Given that I have had to work hard to overcome feelings of failure, criticism, and fear of disappointing others, I find it ironic that I was named Gail. I know my parents chose Gail from a shortlist that included Kathy and Penelope. They didn't anticipate the impact of predictive text that would be the bane of my life in recent years. Every day, I hit the 'f' instead of the 'g' on the Qwerty keyboard on my phone in particular. Guess what happens when you do that? You get the word 'fail'. If you get a text message signed by Fail, it's me...

Limiting beliefs have long-term impacts

There is a well-known parable of a baby elephant confined to a small space for years. The baby elephant will initially try to break the rope. But the rope is too strong, and so it learns it can't break it. It stays in the area defined by the length of the rope. When the elephant grows into a 5-tonne adult that could easily break the rope, it doesn't even try. It has learned as a baby that it can't.

Around the age of 9 or 10, I was in the Brownies. It was there that the seeds of a limiting belief were sown – and contributed to shaping my passion for inclusion. It is one of several events that contributed to a limiting belief that I still work hard on to this day. On a dull Friday afternoon, after school, the Brownies gathered at a campsite. We all lined up to be allocated to a tent for the next two nights. There were six tents, and six Brownies were selected as leaders, and they took turns selecting girls to be in their tent. I was the last girl to be picked.

I felt humiliated and ashamed. I felt left out, isolated, and sad. The girls in the tent where I was put were not friendly. During the night, I asked to be moved to another tent. There was much fuss and disruption, and I felt so self-conscious. I was moved to another tent of girls who already had the advantage of several hours of bonding. It wasn't a pleasant experience. I had spoken up, but the consequences weren't good for me. I formed a belief that I'm better off to just deal with it rather than to speak up. Now I think about how I dealt with my unexpected crap-hand over several years, and I'm sure that I was slow to act because I believed that there was no point in speaking up.

I have held on to feedback from a leader that I admired and respected. Amongst other valued comments, the feedback says: 'Need to build confidence and be confident enough to put a point of view forward in discussions and defend it.' Remember, this feedback was provided to me around thirty-five years after the Brownies camp!

When I was in Grade 3, we all had to audition to be in the school choir. The teacher (I can still see the huge man with an awful moustache and big red face) made his way across the room, squeezing in between the rows of children. We all sang together.

When he got to you, he would put his ear close to your face. If you were not suitable, he poked you in the stomach. Then you sat down. You guessed it. I was poked. I was one of the children who was not good enough. I am self-conscious to this day, and if I can get out of standing close to anyone else while singing, I will.

I've always considered myself plain and too tall. I think this was reinforced in Grade 1 when I was the guiding star in the Christmas nativity play. I spent the entire play standing at the back of the stage, draped in a sheet, holding a foil-covered cardboard star aloft. No talking or movement was required. The teacher could have taped a star on the wall and achieved the same effect!

Limiting beliefs can be overcome

Here's an example of overcoming my limiting beliefs. I remember a day in my childhood. I was sitting on a stool, having my hair done. I was around 9 years old. I remember what I was wearing – a homemade tartan dress that I loved. I said, 'Mum, we live on an island. I'm glad we live on an island. It's special.' My mum responded, 'There are lots of people on this and other islands.' The message I heard was we are not special. You are not special. This compounded the other messages I had heard in my childhood. There were things I had wanted to do. But my requests were always dismissed. Can I join the marching girls? No, that's showing off. Can I attend a high school with a uniform with a hat and stockings and gloves? No, you will be fine at the high school up the road.

But then, in 2014, I was undertaking my Master of Public Administration with a cohort of 100 senior public servants from across Australia and New Zealand. I was the sole Tasmanian. In the afternoon before our first evening session, we found out we had to come up with a presentation for the evening session, presented in our state groups. The Victorians and the New Zealanders were insistent that I join them, so that I wasn't on my own. While I appreciated the offer, I said no. I would go it alone. There I was, back on the stool of my childhood, and finally, I had a chance to have that special moment, where I was the only one from my island of Tasmania in the room. Fired up with adrenaline and pride, I pulled off a presentation that had the room laughing, clapping, and engaged. That limiting belief was crushed. It can be done, my friends.

Seek help if you need it

You might need to dig deep to find the motivation to deal with your limiting beliefs. It might be painful, and you might need to find some external support. In my experience, I have found that guided visualisation and meditation are beneficial. My tip is to test a few out before you subscribe or buy. I need to feel comfortable with the voice of the narrator. If I don't connect with the sound, I can't engage. The voice of Jack Canfield works for me, and you can subscribe to him at www.jackcanfield.com

A completely different voice is that of Carrie Green from the Female Entrepreneur Association and author of *She Means Business*[16]. I also enjoy listening to her.

There are many others. Put 'guided visualisations' into your search engine, and you will find something you are comfortable with.

One guided visualisation that works for me takes me back to a place in my childhood. I look to see who is with me, where I am, what is happening around me. There might be something

---

16   https://www.goodreads.com/en/book/show/30315913-she-means-business

happening that I don't like, or someone might be there that I'm uncomfortable to be with. I notice colour, smell, sound, texture, and feeling in my body. I take note of what I am telling myself. My adult self talks to my younger self, and I help that younger self make a new belief that will be empowering. It might be about life, relationships, acceptance, forgiveness, or something else. I might need to forgive another person from my childhood. I say things like 'I don't like what you did, I don't condone what you did, I understand that you were doing the best you could. I'm willing to forgive you so that I can go free and live the life I want to live.'

When it's time to leave the place I have visualised, I tell my younger self that as an adult, I am always there for them, and I love them. And then I move to the future, to be my wise 90-year-old self. I give my current adult self advice about pressing issues based on all the wisdom of the life that I've lived.

I have also found a Tri-Sync Integration Process useful. See more in Chapter Eleven of Jack Canfield's book *Maximum Confidence: 10 Steps to Extreme Self-Esteem* Audio Program[17]. I found it on Audible. It's different! It might not be for you, but it is useful for me.

---

17   https://www.bookdepository.com/Maximum-Confidence-Jack-Canfield/9780743570015

Personal project 10: Appoint a limiting belief accountability partner

Here is a list of limiting beliefs that are quite common:

- I can't speak in public.
- Boys don't cry.
- People aren't interested in your problems.
- Act like a lady.
- I'm useless on my own.
- It's just my luck!
- I mustn't speak out about THAT issue.
- I'm not as good as him/her/them.
- I'm not a good child; I should be visiting my elderly parents more.
- I'm not loved.
- I am weak if I show my emotions.
- The bank will never lend money to someone like me to buy a house.
- That family across the road is perfect; we aren't.

How many of those can you relate to? Are any of them showing up in your life? How are they showing up? Do you have others to add to the list? Would you like to resolve them?

Identifying them is one thing, but you are going to need the courage to address them. Appoint someone you trust to be your 'limiting belief accountability partner'. Task them with telling you when your limiting beliefs show up. The limiting beliefs might be so ingrained that you don't know they are part of your vocabulary. Every time you get caught out, find something tangible to mark it.

Put a gold coin in a jar. Put a sticker on your calendar. Do anything that will remind you how often you're doing it. Being more conscious is a good start to minimise the impact.

Choose your helpers wisely

You might want to talk to friends about how you're feeling and what you're thinking. When dealing with challenges in your life, be aware that others also have their baggage. In her book *The Gifts of Imperfection*, Brené Brown[18] talks about several reactions you may get from friends when you want to talk things over. Remember that your friends will come to your situation with their assumptions based on their experiences. One friend that you should avoid when you are wanting to talk about limiting beliefs is the one that feels that they should use the opportunity to tell you their story. You'll recognise it when they start with something like: 'That's nothing! Listen to what happened to me!'

What makes you tick

Learning about yourself never ends. It's a bit like peeling an onion. We are all made up of multiple layers, and there is something new to think about and learn at every layer. Some layers come off evenly, and others tear and dig into the next layer when they're

---

18 Brown, B 2010, *The Gifts of Imperfection: Let Go of Who You Think You're Supposed to Be and Embrace Who You Are,* Hazelden Publishing, Minnesota

not supposed to. Putting a different way of being into place is both challenging and rewarding.

I now know that when you know more about yourself, you can do better with your decision-making and make sounder judgements. Your interactions with your colleagues, family, and friends will improve. You will know what your triggers are and how to regulate your responses. You might not like what you find out, but knowledge is power.

As a much older and wiser person with lots of life experience, I know myself better than before. However, the journey continues. I am still learning about myself, and I'm confident I hardly knew me back then. I knew that I was plain, too tall, that there was not too much point speaking up and making a fuss, so I was just agreeable and tried to be a 'good girl'. I knew that I was the big sister and the oldest child and needed to be a helper. And I didn't know that I didn't know me.

I wish I had had more insight into why I thought the way I did and what shaped my behaviours and personality traits. My thoughts about me were superficial but firmly informed by conditioning from the parenting styles and social constructs of the time. I say superficial because, at the time, I just scooped them up with acceptance and didn't think about them, although I now know the impact of those thoughts. They have deep roots and have impacted my life. You will have them too.

My favourite diagnostic tools

There are many tools and assessments available that can help you to understand yourself. Two of my favourites are:

- DISC Advanced® found at www.discprofile.com.au that diagnoses behavioural styles.
- i4 Neuroleader™ Model found at www.aboutmybrain.com that enables you to know which leadership capabilities you could develop further.

DISC Advanced® is a four-quadrant model describing different types of behaviours we all exhibit in the workplace based on the pace at which we typically operate and how we prioritise people or tasks.

The behaviours in all the styles have benefits and challenges that they present to others.

The DISC Advanced® Profile assessment gives an insight into which of the behaviours we tend to exhibit more often, and the combination of traits that makes up our unique style.

It also gives us an understanding of how to recognise and adjust our natural behaviours to interact more effectively. Here's a story that demonstrates what can happen when you are in circumstances where you are feeling uncomfortable and not aligned with your environment.

Through DISC Advanced®, I know that my natural behavioural style in the workplace is that I am patient, I'm loyal, a helper, and cooperative. I like clarity, am firmly values-driven, and I communicate with diplomacy. I am organised and composed. I am what is called a 'high steady'.

However, my adjusted style for one workplace I was in was to focus on results, make fast decisions, be assertive, and value facts over emotions. The expectations were clear that this was the accepted way of working. Any deviation from this style drew disdain.

I achieved outcomes. I performed well. But being in that workplace every day was a stressor to me. I was exhausted by the hour by hour adjustments I needed to make to my natural style. When I recognised the misalignment between my natural and adjusted styles, I was validated to find a different career direction; I had the evidence I needed through undertaking the DISC Advanced® assessment.

The About My Brain Institute has developed the i4 Neuroleader™ Model. This model takes a neuroscience approach to brain and body processes when it comes to leadership and management practices. The model recognises that the world has evolved, and we need to find a way to develop excellent leadership in a volatile, complex, ambiguous, and uncertain world. The assessment process quantifies your performance, collaboration, innovation, and agility. It focuses on the whole person. It includes input from family members and friends, your manager, colleagues, direct reports, and peers. I've completed the assessment twice in the last five years and have found more information about myself each time.

I've learned about the importance of balance. Balance refers to a series of actions and attitudes that help the person's brain perform at its best. I wish I had known many years ago that for balance I needed good supportive social connections to take care of my body and physical condition, and to have a positive attitude to my health and nutrition.

I also learned that I now have much stronger mental readiness. But I needed good mental readiness years ago. Maybe life wouldn't have been quite so difficult if I could do then what I can do now. I'm good at planning, using more positive than negative words when speaking to myself, managing feelings of anxiety even when I don't feel supported, and feeling confident about myself and my abilities.

You might think that you know yourself. You might also be defensive and are saying, 'I don't need anyone else to tell me.' Or 'I've done these things before. They don't know what they're talking about.'

Use a valid, reputable tool. The tools are not designed to show that some people are better than others. They are all about helping you understand yourself. There are no rights or wrongs. Don't be closed to hearing what the tool is telling you; it is an opportunity to grow.

You do need to have a growth mindset to maximise the learnings. Learning might take the form of new knowledge, affirmation, validation, challenging information, to help you make sense of situations and other people.

The process can be challenging, but it's worth it if you are wanting and willing to learn. Use courage. And commit.

Personal project 11: Complete a diagnostic

Where do you want to start to find out some more about yourself? You could contact me to access the diagnostic tool for DISC Advanced®, or the i4 Neuroleader™ Model. Alternatively, you could pop any of the following into a search engine followed by 'diagnostic':

- communication style
- behavioural style

- leadership capabilities
- overall strengths
- personality type
- level of authenticity
- emotional intelligence.

Here's what to do after you have chosen a valid tool:

- Complete it.
- Read the report and highlight what stands out for you.
- Get a debrief (if that's part of the deal).
- Write down some specific actions.
- Show what you've written to a trusted friend, colleague or coach.
- Ask them to check in with you in four weeks and then in three months.

 It's a wise investment. No one is more important than you. When you are the best you can be, you are better for those around you. Remember, you can't drink from an empty cup.

Sometimes these assessments may be a little expensive. You may be able to claim them as a tax deduction. You may be able to negotiate a payment plan. It will be worth it, particularly if you have follow-up coaching sessions. These will help you to be accountable, and to develop and embed new habits.

Talk to your employer about including a diagnostic in your annual performance review plan. There is great benefit in a group of colleagues doing a diagnostic assessment together. You can debrief as a team, develop a team action plan, and have a common language. Team productivity, dynamics, and relationships all improve.

You may be worried about hearing things that you don't want to hear or acknowledge. That's common. One of my clients was happy to do a self-assessment but was nervous about a 360° assessment where he would hear others' views. He was brave, and courage prevailed. He now has a great action plan that helps him to focus on self-care, and to practise collaboration and creativity. He knows that his intuition is worth listening to.

Meet Caitlin.

Caitlin said this about her experience of the i4 Neuroleader™ Model.

> My experience participating in the i4 Neuroleader™ Model with Gail has been exciting, informative and beneficial both personally and in my professional practice. I thoroughly enjoyed completing the survey and unpacking the report, delving into the areas I need to leverage, explore and transform across the four key competencies. I engaged in rich critical self-reflection and then confidently created an individual improvement plan. This influenced my leadership style to focus on delivering clear directions, implement project initiatives and motivate a team to succeed.

Contact me if you want to undertake a DISC Advanced® or i4 Neuroleader™ Model 360° diagnostic.

Be courageous. Invest in you. It is worth it. You are worth it.

Continuing the journey to being unstoppable

Let's add the key messages from this chapter into the diagram – use your knowledge and know yourself.

CHAPTER SEVEN

The dance begins

*You can't stay in your corner of the Forest waiting for others
to come to you. You have to go to them sometimes.*

— AA Milne, *Winnie-the-Pooh*

Dance steps in the zone of conscious grit

Being in the zone of conscious grit can be challenging. I align
that experience with dancing. You need to practise and persist,
tweak as you go, and find the right partners to help you find your
feet and keep you upright. It's not a secure place to be. There
will be casualties, and you need to prepare for injuries to other
people because your decisions will affect others. You will need
both preventative strategies and a first-aid kit.

Being in the zone of conscious grit isn't a neat linear process.
You are on the dance floor with others. Their steps sometimes
take them into your path, and you may or may not appreciate that.

Your actions might take you forward or backwards, or around and around 'til you get dizzy.

In the zone of conscious grit, setbacks will happen, and you will feel disappointed. Sometimes they will feel insurmountable. But in the context of the entire journey you're on, you will look back and appreciate those setbacks for what they are – another opportunity to learn. Recognise this so that you won't be disappointed when you need to go backwards. It's just part of the dance. When you twirl and come back to face the front, and things have changed for the worse, don't be disappointed. That's normal too. There'll also be times when things go beautifully well.

When you think about dancing, there are lots of things that happen which are relevant to thinking about this dance of personal change. Maybe you'll step on your partner's toes. Someone will have polished the floor, and you'll slip and slide. Sometimes there's chewing gum on your shoe, and you don't move quickly or smoothly. You make mistakes. It would help if you oriented yourself to where you are on the dance floor, take your time when learning, dance the steps with care, and practise. When you are going with the flow, the next step seems natural. But just as quickly, the flow changes. When it does, you might twirl around and lose your balance or your orientation.

Dancing can be exhausting

Has this ever happened to you? You go to the supermarket. You are so pleased with yourself. You wrote a list and remembered to take it with you, you stuck to the list and remembered to bring your reusable bags. You took the kids with you and resisted all of their requests for the treats they wanted. There were no tantrums. The dance was going so well. Then when you get to the checkout, you realise you've left your credit card at home. All of a sudden, you are flat on your back on the dance floor. It was going well. And now it's not.

I once made a career decision for reasons I thought were right at the time. I was considering job satisfaction, advancement and finding a role that would stretch my capabilities. I wanted to 'make a difference' in another sector. I did my homework. I sought advice from others. I used my network and found out as much information as I could. I secured a role that I thought was going to be just what I wanted. I was successful in moving to the position.

But it wasn't what I had thought it would be.

The dance floor had a shiny coating that looked beautiful, but it was actually a poisonous layer of toxic relationships and uncivil interaction.

To stay on my feet on that dance floor was a difficult task every day. The dancing steps that I needed to stay authentic and operate within my value set were frantic and complex. No matter how hard I tried, I couldn't learn the dance. I was often stepping on the toes of others. The dance floor was sometimes crowded. At other times, I seemed to be dancing solo. I felt giddy with the flurry of actions that would deliberately bring others to their knees.

I set out to find an alternative dance floor. Whilst I was seeking that, I danced lightly until I could leave that dance, and learn new steps with others where I could make the positive difference I wanted to make.

My original decision and move didn't work out the way I had wanted it to. So I had to regroup and find another way. That is what being in the zone of conscious grit is all about.

Practise your dance steps and form new habits

When you are dancing in the zone of conscious grit, you will be developing new habits. That's not always easy. Have you ever tried to learn salsa or another sequence dance? You may have learned it earlier in your life with a different teacher who had different styles and steps. Now you need to unlearn what you learned before on the dance floor and learn new steps. Then you need to practise them until new habits are formed. It is the determination, persistence, tenacity, and resilience during this unlearning and learning phase that will keep you dancing in the zone of conscious grit. There is a reality though – it is tough for some to stay the course of learning and unlearning. It can sometimes be tempting to give up. Some do.

Think about how many people have determinedly joined weight loss clubs, gyms, and support groups to stop gambling and deal with other addictions. Now think of how many don't succeed. Creating new habits takes time and repetition. It takes all the qualities of being in the zone of conscious grit.

Are you in the right dance?

If your dance steps don't fall into place – despite being in the conscious grit zone – it's time to think about what's going on. There will be a reason that you feel wobbly. Ask yourself these questions:

- Should I persist? If not, why not? If so, why?
- Should I continue to be tenacious? If not, why not? If so, why?

- Is my determination well placed now? If yes, why? If not, why not?
- Am I as resilient as I usually am?
- Is my future focus well served?
- Do I need to change my plan?
- If so, how?

Do you need to change your dancing steps? How? When? Or do you need to get off the dance floor?

Setbacks do happen

You're likely to face a setback in the dance. Any setback can seem like the worst possible thing at the time. You might think about it repeatedly and be obsessed with analysing what's happened. You might be kicking yourself for whatever happened. Lots of successful people must work hard to succeed. Here are a couple of examples.

Did you know that Michael Jordan missed 9,000 shots over his career? He lost 300 games and on two occasions, he missed the winning shot for his team. He says he's failed repeatedly in his life, and that is why he succeeds. Did you know that Walt Disney was fired from his first job because he wasn't creative enough?

Here are a few things you can try if you are experiencing a setback. Firstly, a sense of humour helps. Even though it's the last thing that you feel like doing, laughing will help you release endorphins and dopamine – the feel-good chemicals.

Secondly, remember three tough events you've already been through. You are still standing, aren't you? You may have fallen nine times, but you have stood up ten. What did you do at that time? What did you learn? What can you apply from that learning now?

Dancing with partners is a good thing

It took me a long time to find the value of spending time with others, learning from them, and accepting their help. One of the sayings that I repeatedly heard growing up, which I now realise had an impact on me, was 'They made their bed, now they have to lie in it.' That term was a consistent reinforcement of the limiting belief that I should do things pretty much alone.

Once I worked out that others could help me and our situation, our circumstances improved. When I spoke with the doctor who validated my pain, I gained confidence in trusting others. In *The Power of Vulnerability*, Brené Brown gives a message to all the lone wolves out there. 'No, we can't go it alone. We need support.' She also says that many of us are great at giving help but terrible at asking for help.

I can relate to this.

My natural tendency is to cope alone. You might be the same. But when I allowed other people to help me, I accessed training, employment opportunities, an outlet for my creativity, an increase in confidence, extra cash, and I expanded my contacts.

Here's how my dance partners helped me. Around the time the children were 14 months old and 6 years old, we settled into our home, and I was doing some family day care. Looking after children at home while their parents worked wasn't enough for me financially, and I wasn't challenged in any way. I was ready to study.

Leveraging from my conversation with a GP, I reached out to others.

I rang TAFE Tasmania and enquired about a child care assistant course I had seen advertised. Sometimes the universe works in our favour. The day I phoned, the Head of Childcare Studies picked up the phone. Joan asked me about myself and why I was setting my sights on the assistant course. She felt it was a low bar. I had done well in high school and at matriculation college. She told me that I should consider a higher-level course over two years full time or four years part time. I decided I would do the Associate Diploma course and set about organising child care and giving notice to the parents of children in my family day-care. This was another tipping point in my life. Again, it was validation that got me there.

I embarked on two years of part-time study and then the third year of full-time study. This study was the best thing for me at the time.

I developed an appetite for a career in the early years of work. It wasn't long before I was appointed as the licensee of pre-kindergarten services, providing a program for children aged 3 and 4. I loved my two sessions per week, independently running a program. I juggled this around part-time study and running a playgroup. In the year Alanna was in kindergarten, and Jason was around 10, I studied full time. It was challenging, but it was a great time in my life.

The teachers seemed to enjoy the maturity and life experience that I brought to the class. I was chosen to give the speech on behalf of the students at the graduation ceremony. About ten years ago, I had the opportunity to tell Joan how much her conversation with me had positively impacted my life. She'd listened to my story, validated my potential, challenged my thinking, and recommended a path that made an impact on my future.

I am also grateful to the other mums at Jason's school. When he was in Prep and Alanna was about 2, I saw a few lines in the school newsletter. One of the mums was going to show others how to do applique. I had always loved sewing, and I went along. I was so inspired, and I set about putting an applique on many things, notably Alanna's clothing. People then asked me to decorate clothing for their children. I started making tracksuits and decorating them, and a shop in Richmond, Tasmania, and another in Salamanca Place agreed to sell them.

My clothing was in demand. I got up at four in the morning to cut, iron, stick, and sew before the kids got up, and then we went to study, work, and school — whatever was on that day. Business got so busy that the shop bought me the fleecy fabric in huge rolls. I cut out tracksuits until my hand ached, but I loved the creative process of making applique designs. I also loved that others enjoyed my work enough to pay for it.

I made my swing tags at first — blue cardboard hearts with little stickers on them. The sticker was a pig, and my label was This Little Piggy. I was immensely proud when I graduated from cardboard to embroidered labels.

As adults, my daughter and I often laugh about the tracksuits that I designed and sold. She wore them every day. Not only did they have applique on the front: many had knee and elbow pads edged in appliqued lace. With her side ponytail and matching homemade scrunchie Alanna was the picture-perfect model for my clothing.

While studying full time in the final year at TAFE, I formed strong relationships with many fellow students. Three of us would travel together to the campus and home again. I had an eight-seater van, and with them, myself and the two children, there was lots of chatter as we did pick-ups and drop-offs at various destinations. Studying helped me form friendships and to participate in things that I wouldn't previously have done. It was memory-making stuff.

In terms of my career, I didn't get a start or momentum until I reached out to others. My financial situation improved. I struggled at first, then it was okay, and then it was better than okay. I was also able to go from no qualifications to achieving a Master of Public Administration. I went from casual, to part time, then full time, and permanent frontline roles to the corner office. Being in the zone of conscious grit has its rewards.

Personal project 12: Who would you like on your dance floor?

Make two lists:

- Your natural partners (you may want to refer to the Changemaker Framework. Who did you put in your kitchen cabinet? See Chapter Five).
- The skills and capabilities you want your dancing partners to have.

Then consider:

- Do you need to add other partners?
- Do you have emotional vampires on your list? They suck your energy and enthusiasm. Do you really want them to be a dancing partner?
- Do you have someone there who can help you in practical ways?

- Is there someone that you can have a safe meltdown with – someone who doesn't judge?
- Are all the qualities and capabilities you listed covered?
- If not, where are you going to find them?

Here are some tips to help you reach out and get the help you need:

- Make sure that the person you want to help you knows that you need help. If you're unclear about what you need or are an emotional mess and can't express your needs, you might not get what you need. For example, if you find a dancing partner who sends you cakes and biscuits, but you need a babysitter for an hour on Tuesday morning to go for a swim – tell them!

- Secondly, the person needs to know that you want help. They also need to know that you aren't going to take their time and energy and do nothing with their effort. Don't drown them in detail but let them know that you did follow up on a conversation you had with them – and it worked or didn't work.

- Thirdly, approach your potential helpers individually, not as a group. If you approach a group by email, some people will leave the task to others. Individual approaches, based on what each can bring to your situation, is the better way to go. Don't send a group email to the family asking them to stack the five tonnes of firewood in the driveway. Make a direct request to the person who is best placed – and then go to plan B or C if you need to.

- Finally, don't ask a potential helper for something that they simply can't give you. If someone is going through a difficult situation themselves, they won't have the emotional reserves to listen to you. But they might be able to give you some apples from their tree.

You may have had a poor experience with people who you thought would be the right partners. There's a little saying that 'Other women will straighten your crown'. I call BS on that one. They might, or they might not. Any individual can support you, or not. There have been some fabulous women who have helped me through my working life and some remarkable men. There have been others whom I haven't enjoyed working with — both men and women. I don't think it relates to gender. I just hope that individuals will reach out and give a hand to others.

Dancing injuries

In Chapter Six, you learned about the human instincts related to thinking and feeling that are hard-wired. Injuries will come from both you and others putting emotion before reason, using first impressions to classify, and seeking to avoid loss. You need to be ready and anticipate what the injuries might be. Prevention is best if you can manage it, but you also need to have the first-aid kit available. You can recover, and you can help other people to heal.

The pace of the dance will be fast and then slow and then fast and then slow. You are going to fall. It's the getting up that makes us stronger. It's inevitable that you fall and get hurt when you learn to walk, ride a bike, or swim. It's no different if you are dancing. Be prepared.

Some of our injuries

My children didn't deserve our crap-hand, and neither did their father. They were injured because of the decisions that I made. Jason's school photo from his Prep class tells the entire story. I still have the picture, and it breaks my heart when I look at it – a sad little boy with shoulders down and head bowed. Then I compare that to a photo of the three of us when he was 10, and Alanna was 5 – confident, smiling, head up, and loving life. I know that somewhere along the line I did apply some first aid. For him, it was making sure that he was able to participate in sporting activities. For Alanna, her world just chugged along. Her father would talk to her when he dropped off or picked up Jason. That seemed to be enough for her at that time in her life. She didn't know any other way of living.

Peter died suddenly in 2000 and I failed to manage the situation. I failed dramatically. Alanna was 13, and Jason was 18. I hadn't prepared the children in any way; I just didn't anticipate this would occur. Peter wasn't living a healthy life and I wish that I had anticipated the possibility of an early death and acted accordingly.

Further, my first-aid kit was not well equipped. The story of how we dealt with that is perhaps for another book. Let's just say for now that some wounds don't ever heal. His death was another reminder that I had let Peter and the children down. I saw the impact on the children. According to my assessment from an archetype diagnostic, I am a warrior, healer, and advocate. But I felt I had failed on all fronts.

This is where the concept of zones is evident. For some time after his death I was on the edge of the zone of conscious grit. I needed to work hard — on myself and my responses — to get back to somewhere near the sweet spot of the zone of conscious grit.

I don't want to speak for Jason and Alanna about how Peter's sudden death impacted them. However, I know from my studies and work with children, families, and childhood trauma that the death of a parent is a shattering experience for an adolescent. That's true for all families. We had unique complications because of our circumstances. As a result of the death of a parent, teenagers' lives are under reconstruction. It is a big deal for them.

Grief is complicated, and grieving was a natural expression of the feelings that my children held for Peter. Both Jason and Alanna grieved. A lot. In different ways. All I could do was be gentle and compassionate in all my efforts to help — regardless of how the grief showed itself.

Prevention

There is a common saying, 'Prevention is better than cure.'

In the context of dealing with life, each of us needs to find the activities, interactions and way of living that help us do our best. Often this is referred to as self-care. When you are effective in your self-care, you can react quickly, read situations, act accordingly, be at your most resilient best, and be focused enthusiastically on the future.

At the time when I needed my self-care to be robust, it was ordinary. There's a lot of unhelpful media and external pressure that suggests self-care is about going to the spa, having a massage, getting your nails done, having a luxury weekend away, or a fancy night out. My budget didn't extend to those things. It has taken me many years to realise that self-care needs to be more grounded than that.

Recently, I found a piece from Brianna Wiest, called 'Self-care is often a very unbeautiful thing'.[19] In this excerpt she says:

True self-care is not salt baths and chocolate cake … it often means looking your failures and disappointments square in the eye and re-strategizing. It is not satiating your immediate desires. It is letting go. It is choosing new. It is disappointing some people. It is making sacrifices for others. It means being the hero of your life, not the victim. It means rewiring what you have until your everyday life isn't something you need therapy to recover from. It is no longer choosing a life that looks good over a life that feels good. It is giving the hell up on some goals so you can care about others. It is being honest even if that means you aren't universally liked. It is meeting your own needs so you aren't anxious and dependent on other people. It is becoming the person you know you want and are meant to be.

This speaks to me; I recommend you read the whole piece.

Keeping yourself as healthy and well as you can is a good investment in preventing, or at least limiting damage when times are tougher than others.

First aid

If an injury has occurred, then you need first aid. There are many things that you can try. You can focus on making others who are injured feel safe, being calm, keeping them engaged in life

---

19   https://thoughtcatalog.com/brianna-wiest/2017/11/this-is-what-self-care-really-means-because-its-not-all-salt-baths-and-chocolate-cake/

and talking about what's happened. You can listen to them and acknowledge how they are feeling. Don't worry about knowing exactly the right thing to say.

Accept that sometimes there is no right thing.

As with me, after Peter's death, sometimes being there is all you can do.

Personal project 13: Get your prevention and first-aid kits ready

Access your template at
www.everywhensolutions.com.au/resources

 It's worthwhile thinking about this in two parts — a prevention strategy, and a first-aid strategy. Think about all the people that might be injured. What can you do to prevent that? How is your self-care? What will you have in your first-aid kit?

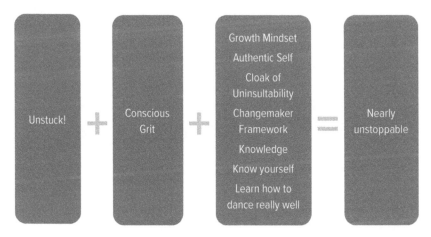

Unstuck! + Conscious Grit + Growth Mindset / Authentic Self / Cloak of Uninsultability / Changemaker Framework / Knowledge / Know yourself / Learn how to dance really well = Nearly unstoppable

PART THREE

CHAPTER EIGHT

The zone of conscious grit and the right brain

Logic will take you from A to B. Imagination will take you everywhere. Creativity is intelligence having fun.

— Einstein

The brain

We need right brain capabilities to function optimally in a world that is volatile, uncertain, complex and ambiguous. This type of world is known as the VUCA world (a term coined in 1987 and based on US leadership theories). When you are in the zone of conscious grit, the right brain capabilities of curiosity, adaptability and resilience will serve you well.

The theme of how the brain functions has been consistent in my adult life. I studied psychology at college. I learned a lot about acquired brain injuries by sharing Peter's journey. When I was in the early childhood sector, I supported research that became more publicly available about how we influence the healthy brain development of children pre- and post-birth. Recently, I've been interested in research around neuroscience and neuroplasticity. It tells us that adults can learn to behave and think differently. We create new neural pathways and strengthen existing neural pathways by thinking and acting in ways relative to the trait that we want to develop.

Ironically, this book leverages from my story about the impact of an acquired brain injury – and I've told you how bad it was. Yet now I'm going to tell you how the brain can re-wire, and new habits can be created. Unfortunately, this doesn't mean that all brain damage can be repaired. For nearly all patients who live through a severe brain injury, permanent, irreversible damage results – and that sadly was Peter's circumstance.

Life isn't easy, even if you have the best environment and the best relationships. Each time we experience an emotion such as anger or frustration, we reinforce that neural pathway. Similarly, when we experience empathy or happiness, that neural pathway is reinforced. We can choose which pathways we want to develop.

It's now established that there are two sides to our brain and each has a specific function. The left brain provides the capacity for us to do things including to think analytically and be logical, and to use facts, be able to sequence and use language, reasoning, science, and mathematics. The right brain provides us with the capacity to be creative and collaborate, and to use imagination, emotion, intuition, and insight.

Being in the zone of conscious grit requires us to use our left and right brains. But given that the world we live in is ever-changing, volatile, uncertain, complex, and ambiguous, there is an increasing need for humans to use their right brain.

It's essential to develop and acquire skills and knowledge that will help you in the future, wherever your life takes you. In my language, that means to get grittier within the zone of conscious grit. You can do this by developing your right brain capability. In her book *Leadership Is Upside Down*, scientist and author Silvia Damiano[20] from the About My Brain Institute uses research and evidence from the field of neuroscience to explain that to be performing optimally, individuals need to have a high level of competency in right brain activities. Right brain leaders who are both leading self or leading others can inspire and motivate.

Damiano says that we need four capabilities to deal with the challenges of the VUCA environment:

- imagination to deal with volatile conditions that are generated by continuous change
- inspiration to overcome the uncertainty created by unpredictable circumstances
- a balanced and integrated brain to realise the connections between different variables in this complex world
- intuition to resolve the ambiguity of our times in which the sequence of simple and linear cause-and-effect no longer work.

These are all right brain traits.

Damiano has created the i4 Neuroleader™ Model (www. aboutmybrain.com) that describes the abilities, traits and

---

20   https://aboutmybrain.com/books

behaviours needed to meet imagination, intuition, integration, and inspiration. The good news is that you can learn these.

Optimal conscious grit uses right brain capabilities

When you are in the zone of conscious grit, you might be on the edge of the zone or right in the middle – let's say that's the sweet spot.

When we deliberately develop right brain traits, we get closer to being in that sweet spot. The attributes are connected and work together to help us innovate, inspire, imagine, and integrate. Here's a simple example.

You are in the zone of conscious grit. You also have a strong capability in the areas of curiosity and adaptability. Here is an example. You have pie served up to you. When the pie is too hot to eat, you adapt and wait 'till it cools. When you are served a piece that's too small to match your appetite, you figure how you will either complement the small serve or shift your thinking to be satisfied with only that much. When it's not your favourite flavour, you have an open mind and try it anyway. You are curious about the taste, texture, and how it goes with the pastry of the pie and the ice cream on the side.

At the end of the experience, you've eaten pie and feel satisfied – even though you didn't get as much pie as you wanted, and it was a flavour that wasn't your favourite. You embraced the challenge and stretched yourself to try a new experience. You've shown you are in a growth mindset.

If the right brain traits of curiosity and adaptability weren't being used in this scenario, you would still be hungry. You would also be blaming others for cutting a small piece of pie and not having your favourite flavour on hand. You would be demonstrating that you have a fixed mindset – not a growth mindset.

In this chapter, I will tell you why it's worthwhile developing robust neural pathways related to curiosity, adaptability, and resilience – and how to go about it.

Curiosity

Former First Lady Eleanor Roosevelt said, 'I think, at a child's birth, if a mother could ask a fairy godmother to endow it with the most useful gift, that gift would be curiosity.'

The word curious means to know there are things we don't know, to explore, and to investigate. Being curious helps us make sense of our world.

We often use the idiom, 'Curiosity killed the cat.' It has a negative connotation and discourages people from being curious. But this is only half the phrase. The original phrase is 'Curiosity killed the cat, but satisfaction brought it back.' The full expression encourages curiosity.

In her book *Cracking the Curiosity Code: The Key to Unlocking Human Potential*, Diane Hamilton[21] says that 'Our bodies are programmed to be curious and reward us when we exercise that curiosity. It is our body's way of encouraging us to find new sources

---

21   Hamilton D 2019, *Cracking the Curiosity Code*, Dr Diane Hamilton, LLC, USA

of food, new means of protecting ourselves, and new ways to aid us in times of crisis.'

Curiosity is a capability that we need to use in the VUCA world. Curiosity is the desire to learn about something or someone. How you go about it and how you persist with it will determine the level of curiosity that you have and the level of benefit that you get from being curious. You might be curious about what happens in the next chapter of a book, so you'll turn the paper over and have a quick flick through, but if you want to understand what's happening and make meaning of it, you'll sit and read it. You might even do some additional research around some of the concepts that have come up.

Curiosity is a natural inclination. Psychologist Jean Piaget described children as 'amateur scientists'. Kids ask 300 or 400 questions a day. As a parent, if you're on the receiving end of those, you get a bit sick of it. But curiosity is a normal and healthy thing. Babies are born curious. Newborns stare into the eyes of an adult. Older infants pull the hair of another child or try to take your glasses off. Toddlers want to pick up, taste, and touch everything they find around the place.

We understand the obvious, curious questioning of 3- and 4-year olds. Asking questions and being curious as an adult is a capability that we need, to find out about the world around us, find solutions, and contribute to problem-solving and innovation.

As adults, we need to inspire curiosity in children — not shut it down. But you may be an adult who was discouraged from being curious as a child. Maybe you come from a family where 'Children need to be seen and not heard.' Perhaps you heard, 'I'm sick of answering your questions' and 'Don't touch.' These may lead to limiting beliefs, as we discussed in Chapter Six. If that's you, you will need to work deliberately on being curious.

When we are not curious, we start to make assumptions and jump to conclusions. Anger can get in the way of curiosity. Curiosity is a precursor to empathy. Those with high levels of curiosity are motivated to imagine the thoughts or state of others. When that happens, you may feel what they feel, and that creates empathy.

Curiosity can be learned

In managing my circumstances, I had to be curious. I was curious about how to survive on limited money, about study and career options, and school options. Being curious is one of the capabilities that I have taken from my unexpected crap-hand experience. When I am curious and looking to innovate or solve problems, I am purposeful. I gain satisfaction when I am doing something purposeful and making a difference. I have learned that being curious provides rewards. It's one of my strengths to this day.

Meet the curious Gail.

I worked for many years in an executive role as manager of services in the early-years sector. I was committed to the sector overall and was chair of the State's peak body for early-years services. As employers and managers, we were struggling with getting quality trained staff. And I felt it was time for a job change. So, I got curious. I resigned from my permanent role and took a six month contract with another organisation. I aimed to find out what the reasons were and if I could find some solutions. Was it a problem with the training provider, the training package, the training methodology, the level of support from employers, or something else?

The teaching team I was responsible for doubled the output of students studying the qualifications that the sector needed, and we innovated delivery models. I was curious, and I stayed with the training provider for fourteen years. I moved out of the early-years area. I was responsible for a wide variety of teaching areas not familiar to me, including agriculture, hairdressing, and international education.

I moved into the corporate sector of organisational development, business development, operations, and undertook several periods in the role of chief executive officer. I wouldn't have had those opportunities if I hadn't been curious. I also know that it took courage to be curious. While I'm not providing you with a compelling list of opportunities I've had, I hope that you get the message that curiosity can serve you well.

You may be only a bit curious or not curious at all. You might think that you can't build your curiosity, but curiosity can be learned by doing simple things to strengthen that neural pathway. You can think about where you've never been before and go there. Try an unfamiliar restaurant. Try a different genre of books.

As well as the development of your neural pathways, there are other benefits from being curious. You might think that your kids will not play together nicely in the park. Be curious, give it a go. You might find relationships develop as they find ways to play together in a different environment.

The alternative is that you stay at home with cranky kids who are tired of each other and their usual playthings. Being curious can lead to happiness. Try it.

Curiosity in the workplace

Are you as curious at work as you are at home? At home, you might try out decorating or 'DIY' projects, get creative with cooking, or see if you like a particular sport.

In contrast, the work environment might stifle your curiosity. For all sorts of reasons, you may not ask questions or find out about your colleagues. Remember that in Chapter Four you learned about the benefits of being in a growth mindset. Growth mindset and curiosity are aligned. A big part of being in a growth mindset is to embrace challenges and stretch yourself. It's hard to do if you are not curious about possibilities.

Being curious at work helps you get noticed positively. It will also reinforce your value. You will be a problem solver and a shaper of future actions. Compare these hypothetical scenarios.

Miss Not-Curious goes to her boss and says, 'We have run out of PPE, and the supplier won't have any more for six weeks.'

Miss Curious goes to her boss and says, 'We have run out of PPE, and the supplier won't have any more for six weeks. I've enquired around our other sites, and we have some PPE we can move to get us through the next two weeks. I've made some phone calls and found another supplier who will be a bit more expensive but can supply us so that everyone will be safe. The PPE is of good quality.'

Miss Curious showed several traits. A significant one is curiosity. She was curious to find a solution. As a result, she has been an innovative problem solver.

PS. I'd be motivated to keep her on my team!

Curiosity can be overdone

Like many traits, curiosity can be overdone, and there might be negative consequences. Be aware not to let your curiosity take you down an unhealthy rabbit hole.

Asking too many questions of a personal nature, or delving into documents or databases that you don't need to access are examples where being too curious can get you into trouble. Similarly, looking over your shoulder as you pass by an accident scene is a dangerous use of curiosity.

You need to keep a balance between curiosity and certainty. If you ask too many questions just because you're trying to demonstrate curiosity, you can sow seeds of doubt. You don't want to ask so many questions that people around the table suddenly doubt if something is going to work.

You might be curious about how far you can explore a topic, but you may need to put some limits around your curiosity for the benefit of other people; if eyes are glazing over, it's probably time to stop!

Be aware that curiosity can present as being nosy and associated with gossip. Think about the style you are using. You can be curious without interrogating someone.

Personal project 14: Nurturing your positive curiosity

These are things you can do to strengthen your neural pathways of curiosity:

- Pick a topic and find out as much as you can about it.

- Replace judgemental thoughts with non-judgemental thoughts. For example, instead of 'Their garden is a disgrace,' try, 'I wonder why they can't manage their garden – it might be illness, money, lack of know-how.'

- Work on tolerating uncertainty. It's okay not to know all the facts. It's okay to be in the 'figuring out' stage.

- Don't assume a fact or an outcome; it might not be right.

- Change angry thoughts like 'I can't (expletive) believe you are doing that' to 'I wonder why you are acting like that?' When you think in this way, your curiosity will generate empathetic thoughts.

- Read books, join a book club where you can discuss what you read.

- Use the 'Five Why' questions (later in this chapter) to get to the bottom of an issue.

- Always look for learning opportunities; they are all around you.

- Know that asking questions or looking for information is not a sign of weakness.

Don't let your curiosity be stifled

Curiosity can get stifled by many things. Being curious takes courage. Let's say you want to learn to play the guitar. You don't have the money. Find the courage to rearrange your budget so that you can. Remember from Chapter Six that your response will shift the outcome. Make adjustments to your budget and you CAN learn to play the guitar.

Some people might find your questions and curiosity annoying. Use your knowledge from Chapter Six about hard-wired humans to understand that those people are likely reacting to their hard-wired instincts. For example, they might be hearing the negative first; they have heard your questions and assumed that you are trying to catch them out, or that you don't believe them. When you understand that, you can preface your curiosity with 'You know so much more about this topic than I do – can I ask you a few questions?'

Stay confident that you are being curious with good intent, so treat any barriers that come up as small setbacks and courageously push through as you would do in a growth mindset.

Adaptability

Adaptability is the ability to adjust direction, adjust course, adjust your strategy, and adjust how you're going to do things according to what's happening around you. Adaptability helps you find solutions to challenges. You might experiment with adapting a response that isn't entirely fit for purpose, for example. Alongside curiosity, it is another element of demonstrating that you have a growth mindset.

Being adaptable is a crucial competency, particularly in times of immense change. In her TED Talk, *3 Ways to Measure Your Adaptability – and How to Improve It,* Natalie Fratto[22] says adaptability is a 'must have' trait. She says that 'Everyone has the

---

22 https://ideas.ted.com/these-days-adaptability-is-a-must-have-trait-heres-how-to-spot-it-and-increase-it/

capacity to measure, test, and improve their ability to adapt to new circumstances.'

Being adaptable was a critical factor in a successful cave rescue. In June 2018, a soccer team was trapped deep in caves in Thailand. The story of their rescue is inspiring and told in the book *Against All Odds*[23] by Craig Challen and Richard Harris. They needed to do many things, including building trust within a large multi-skilled team, remain calm under pressure, and constantly adapt to changing circumstances. In their story, they describe how all aspects of their challenge continually changed: the water, the equipment, the quality of the equipment, the makeup of the team, the condition of the boys stuck in the cave, their own physical health, and the method of rescue. Before entering, they were told, 'I just want to warn you. You're going to dive to the end of the cave. You're going to see these kids. They're all looking healthy and happy and smiley. Then, you're going to swim away, and they're probably all going to die.'

Challen and Harris entered the cave with a growth mindset. They were prepared to embrace the challenges in front of them and stretch themselves to do the best job they could. They adapted their actions, their interactions, and their emotions to succeed.

It was not only Challen and Harris who needed to be adaptable. They describe how the Thai Navy SEALS turned out to be 'the greatest babysitters ever', and the team's assistant coach displayed 'incredible devotion and a deep, spiritual calm'.

Silvia Damiano says that there are three elements needed for adaptability – versatility, dealing with uncertainty, and self-

---

23 https://www.penguin.com.au/books/against-all-odds-9781760899455

correction. Challen and Harris used all of these in the rescue, as did the entire team.

A person who is not adaptable will say, 'Oh, okay, it's not going so well. In six weeks, I'll review and do something different.' An adaptable person will be 'on the ball', thinking about how to change things, and will be flexible and nimble.

Like curiosity, adaptability is not something that you are necessarily born with, but it is something that you can learn. It's a life skill, like learning to ride a bike or ice-skate, or to garden well. Like curiosity, adaptability is underpinned by courage.

We're more adaptable than we think we are. Writing this book during a pandemic has given me examples of adaptability. Many of my friends and family are working from home. Restaurants have adapted to take-away and dine-at-home options. Kids are doing their dance lessons via Zoom or Skype. Farmers who usually sell things at the market are packaging them up in boxes and selling them at their farm gate. Family and friends are connecting into live streams of funeral services, and there's even a drive-through wedding service. Many children have returned to playing sport with some changes: netballs are sanitised at the end of every quarter; there is no handshaking at the end of the game; and spectators are limited to two per player. But netball continues.

Meet Anna.

Operations Manager Anna has enabled her staff to work from home. There is no disruption to clients, and work health and safety issues related to workstations have been resolved. Her team members are happy. They feel trusted and are productive. They also feel safe and appreciate that they and Anna have worked together and adapted. Their ability to adapt has now led to innovation. They realised that customers don't need face-to-face service for all interactions. Clients welcome responsive phone service. Anna's courage underpinned her willingness to be adaptable, and there have been rewards for staff and clients.

Here's a simple example of my adaptability.

A couple of years ago, in preparation for my family Christmas lunch of around thirty-five people, I decided to buy a deep fryer. I wanted to plug it on outside to quickly cook chips and finger food that would soak up the alcohol later in the day when people stayed and had a few drinks. The sales assistant at the shop told me to forget a deep fryer and get an air fryer. Given that he didn't have any deep fryers in stock anyway, I was suspicious, but he told me how he used and loved his air fryer. I bought one. It is now an essential appliance in our kitchen, and I've adapted most things that I would usually cook in the oven to the air fryer. I might even buy another one!

Meet Billie.

Billie is involved in developing the marketing campaign for the annual intake of students of an education facility. For years she has put up posters, advertised through television and radio campaigns, and used social media. The age demographics in the catchment area have changed and there is a large multicultural population. Intake numbers dropped. Billie adapted her strategy – she unlearned what she already knew. She used her networks to find potential students and overcame language barriers impacting on the enrolment process. Intake numbers improved.

Seeking perfection can hold you back

One of the things that can hold you back from being adaptable is the trait of perfectionism. The link might not seem obvious, but perfectionists are not good at adapting because they're terrified that they're going to make mistakes. They are worried that their planning isn't perfect and there will need to be changes. Often perfectionists become overwhelmed when something out of the ordinary happens. They are unable to adapt because they are scared that they're going to make a mistake. The risk is too much for them to deal with.

Forbes contributor and psychotherapist Susanna Mittermaier[24] writes about two types of perfectionists: the adaptive and the maladaptive.

Adaptive perfectionism means that even if you strive for perfection, you still accept some leeway to get it wrong and try again. Maladaptive perfectionism is more toxic. It's the type of perfectionism where people constantly criticise themselves and others. They feel the need to control all aspects of their life and what's happening around them.

Personal project 15: 'Ask the Five Why' questions

Here's a technique that will help you to think about things in different ways.

---

24 https://www.forbes.com/sites/womensmedia/2018/08/14/
    how-to-free-yourself-from-perfectionism-and-activate-greater-
    success/?sh=67dfef9c3da1

You might want to jump straight to a particular thought or action, but if you slow down and use these questions, you can adapt your next steps to be more appropriate, more productive, more conducive to good relationships. Here is a simple example. You have twenty people coming for a BBQ tomorrow. You go out for the afternoon to get supplies and expect that the adults in the house are going to mow the lawn. You come home, and the lawn isn't mowed. Your standard response might be to get angry and scream, 'Why hasn't the (expletive) lawn been mowed?' Using the 'Ask the Five Why' questions, you can take a different approach:

Why 1. Why hasn't the lawn been mowed? The mower won't work.

Why 2. Why won't the mower work? It's run out of oil.

Why 3. Why has it run out of oil? Because there's a leak in the hose.

Why 4. Why is there a leak in the hose? Because the hose split.

Why 5. Why did the hose split? Because the mower has been left out in the yard all winter.

By this time, you've generated an understanding of what happened. You've adapted your response to bring forth information to solve the problem, rather than have an angry argument. (Of course, the lawn still isn't mowed – and you still might be angry.)

And here's another personal project to develop neural pathways to improve adaptability.

Use open-ended questions that stimulate your brain to think about possible scenarios. Don't be afraid to make these 'what if' questions fairly wild because you're trying to get your brain thinking about how to solve these crises. They might include things like, 'What if all my revenue from my business just stopped?' 'What if my shop's front doors got locked, we couldn't get them opened for two weeks, and customers couldn't come in?' What if your internet went down for a month? What if the entire police force got COVID-19? What if we couldn't buy flour, eggs, and milk for a whole month? What other scenarios can you think of that test your thinking? What solutions can you think of?

Here's a simple example of adaptability and courage. A friend was telling me that she had bought all the ingredients to make a cake. It was a new recipe she hadn't tried. It was called a Strawberry Cream cake and had strawberries and cream cheese in it. When she went to bake it, she found she had bought a chive cream cheese. She added it – the cake was delicious!

Emotional resilience

Resilience is a term often used. Australian Prime Minister Scott Morrison referred to it repeatedly in an address to the National Press Club[25] on 29 January 2020.

His address included sixteen references to 'resilience'. They included the economy, natural disasters, a changing climate and other unspecified threats. He said that mitigation and adaptation both contribute to resilience, he spoke of national resilience, practical action on climate resilience and adaptation, and asserted that farmers are on the front line of resilience.

25　https://www.pm.gov.au/media/address-national-press-club

There is a large body of literature on community and personal resilience, traversing disciplines such as psychology, sociology, engineering, geography and management.

So, what is this thing called resilience?

Dictionary.com defines resilience as:

- the power or ability of a material to return to its original form, position, after being bent, compressed, or stretched, elasticity
- the ability of a person to adjust to, or recover from, illness, adversity, major life changes, buoyancy
- the ability of a system or organisation to respond to or recover from, a crisis or disruptive process.

There are times, however, when returning to original form is not the best thing. For example, even though I demonstrated resilience in dealing with Peter's illness, I wasn't able to return our family situation to its original form. However, I believe that I was resilient, in line with the second dot point above.

In the context of this book, I'm using the analogy often used in the field of psychology. That is, of bouncing back. I talk about resilience as the ability to adapt to stressful situations or crises and to bounce back. It's relevant to both severe challenges and minor stresses that happen in everyday life. Psychologists say that resilience is the most important factor in mental health, performance and success. People who are resilient to adversity, difficulty, and stress do well in life.

We all have stuff that happens in life. Emotional resilience is constructive for managing those situations in the best way possible. Having resilience doesn't mean that you don't struggle or make mistakes. It doesn't mean that you don't need to ask for help. It means that you keep bouncing back, using others that you trust to help as you need it.

I love this quote, 'I bent until I damn near broke. But that's the thing about resilience. It shows up just as your soul begins to cry, and catapults your strength into overdrive.' (source unknown)

This thing called life is a swirling, gurgling, sucking, boiling cauldron of life's challenges, catalyst moments, and opportunities to learn. I can't imagine anyone having a life where a level of resilience isn't required.

Moments that require resilience happen all the time in our lives. You know them. You've experienced them — the knot in the stomach, the ache in your heart. These moments become woven into the fabric of your life, creating a unique tapestry that can inspire and guide you in the future. But at the time, you hate them. You are in pain.

Life events are learning opportunities. While they can be painful, they're gold in terms of learning. I like to call them catalyst moments. They don't have to be big things. They are anything that challenges you or disrupts you — for example, changing jobs, moving house, changing your children's school, bringing a puppy into the home, resuming study, becoming ill, or losing your driver's licence for three months. In the workplace, it might even be when you are asked (or told) to move offices or desks, or when a new boss arrives on the scene.

A catalyst moment can also come from something positive. Every time you deal with a new situation or a change in circumstances, you learn. When you learn and are open to learning, you are building up resilience. I like to think that you are building resilience muscles. Like developing other muscles, the more you use them, the better they are.

Catalyst moments are not the same as tipping points. In the context of my model, catalyst moments happen within the zones of unconscious and conscious grit. A tipping point happens when you are stuck in unconscious grit and need to get unstuck.

Some people are born with a predisposition to be less upset by changes, difficulties, and surprises. Resilient people use strengths and skills to cope and recover from problems and challenges. The good news is that all of us can develop resilience to some degree through effort and practice.

Resilient people explain what they are going through, but with a coating of positivity. We've all seen bushfire victims interviewed in the aftermath of catastrophic bushfires. Often their resilience is evident – 'We've lost everything we own, but we have each other, and we will be okay.'

If you are resilient, you will:

- be more aware of the emotions you are feeling and why you are feeling them
- persevere, be action-oriented and not give up when faced with obstacles
- believe you are in control of yourself
- have an optimistic outlook
- see positives in most situations
- know the value of support from others
- laugh at life's difficulties
- learn from your mistakes.

If you are not resilient, you may see these signs:

- often feeling overwhelmed
- a tendency to dwell on problems
- using unhealthy coping mechanisms to deal with challenges.

Michelle Obama[26], in her book, *Becoming*, says, 'You should never view your challenges as a disadvantage. Instead, it's important for you to understand that your experience facing and overcoming adversity is actually one of your biggest advantages.'

Here is another story from my garden.

There is a wishing well in my garden. It was made by my dad some years ago. It is about a metre tall, has a peaked roof and a round well. It was forgotten for many years and languished behind a shed next to a small fuchsia.

Now that small fuchsia has become big and is flourishing; its flowers and foliage are beautiful in its flowering season. I grew it from a cutting from a plant that was in my grandmother's backyard. I took the cutting in about 1988, and she would have planted it twenty years before that. It's old, and it has adapted to its circumstances, seasons and suburbs and various levels of care and attention.

Earlier this year, I noticed that in its attempt to grow and find as much sun as possible, some of its branches had pushed through the roof of the wishing well.

Some would see the roof as a barrier. But not this plant. This story reflects many things you need to do when faced with a challenge:

---

26 Obama, M 2018 *Becoming* (Unabridged), Random House Audio Publishing New York

- Keep growing.
- Find a space for you.
- Use that space to push forward.
- Reach for the sunlight, the good times.
- Don't hurt others on the way.
- Find a way to get the light and water you need.
- Reflect the rewards of your efforts.

Not all balls bounce

Was I resilient when in the zone of unconscious grit? I believe I was 'somewhat resilient'. You might relate to feeling this way. In those five years:

- I was aware of the emotions I was feeling and why I was feeling them
- I persevered and was action-oriented, but it was on a day-to-day basis
- I didn't give up when faced with an obstacle.

The description of resilience as being the ability to bounce back might sound flippant; I don't mean it to be. For me, 'bouncing' conjures up images of bouncing balls on a pavement. Bouncing back doesn't always happen easily or at all. It depends on what the balls are made of. Those beautiful glass artisan balls used for decorating don't bounce. Christmas baubles don't bounce. Lindt chocolate balls don't bounce. Rubber balls do bounce.

The message from me is to be a rubber ball. That rubber ball needs to be a bit chewed by the family dog and have a few grass stains embedded into its coating. It needs to have a history. It's been hidden behind the lounge, or a tree in the garden. That type of rubber ball has learned from its previous lessons. It has bite marks to prove it. It still functions effectively as a rubber ball. It still bounces back.

The term 'bounce back' in some ways implies it's a simple action. It's not.

Being resilient is bouncing back repeatedly. When you hit the pavement, you need to be ready to bounce again. So yes, to be resilient is to bounce back, but please don't think it's going to be a nice, neat bounce that takes you straight to the dizzy heights of a new life with no hiccups along the way. Resilient people have common sense to know that challenges will keep coming. Keep treating them as catalyst moments, as learning moments.

I read this somewhere: 'She believed she could, but she was tired. So she rested. The world went on, and it was okay; she knew she could try again tomorrow. And she did.'

That is what resilience is.

You might not relate to the definitions of resilience as I've described them so far. You might relate to this quote from Elizabeth Gilbert[27], author of many books, including *Eat, Pray, Love*. She says, 'The women whom I love and admire for their strength and grace did not get that way because shit worked out. They got that way because shit went wrong, and they handled it. They handled it a thousand different ways on a thousand different days, but they handled it. Those women are my superheroes.'

This description is a realistic one of resilience as I have experienced it.

---

27   https://www.goodreads.com/quotes/7335297-the-women-i-love-and-admire-for-their-strength-and

The big question, then, is how do you get to be one of those women or men? How do everyday people strengthen their capacity to respond well to setbacks and persist in the face of failure rather than give up? How do they cope with the stress of what they are going through?

Articles and books will tell you to 'have a positive mindset and develop the ability to manage pressure'. Let's be realistic. These words are useful but can provide a false sense of security. Even the most resilient people will feel down, anxious, or stressed at some times. The ability to be resilient grows from being in touch with what it's like to fail, from understanding the pain of loss, and from the desperation of being overwhelmed, confused, frustrated, and lost.

In their book *Resilience: The Science of Mastering Life's Greatest Challenges*, professors Charney and Southwick[28] say that 'Resilience is the complex product of genetic, psychological, biological, social and spiritual factors.' They go on to say that our brains can be trained to become more resilient.

There are many activities you can do to train your brain to become more resilient. You'll find lots of information in books and on the internet. I've made a list of those that make the most sense to me:

- Find a sense of purpose.
- Be positive and realistic about the negative aspects of what's going on.
- Know what you stand for.
- Stay true to your values.
- Get a network of supportive, sensible people around you.

---

28 https://www.researchgate.net/publication/287349470_Resilience_The_
science_of_mastering_life's_greatest_challenges

- Know that you might take a new direction — be flexible.
- Don't ignore the problem — be confident that you have the skills and abilities to deal with it.
- Make time to do things you like to do.
- Don't live every minute of every day 'solving the problem'.
- Set goals and plan.
- Know that even little steps forward are helpful.

There are some events in life where you may need external support or professional assistance. If that's you, don't hold back. Ask for it and use it. Any advice or techniques you get will build your resilience muscles for the rest of your life.

Stocktake your catalyst moments

Earlier I described catalyst moments as anything (negative or positive) that challenges or disrupts you when you're in the zones of unconscious or conscious grit. I have had so many I've lost count! But I do know that the neural pathway related to my resilience has been reinforced repeatedly. It's solid now. It wasn't in my teens or early 20s. Like many, I experienced disappointments, conflicts, and frustrations in not being chosen for the roles I wanted.

I watched as my mum's life was sucked away by the insidious impact of multiple sclerosis and Parkinson's Disease. I lost my parents and mother-in-law in a short space of time, had loved pets die, felt helpless as my kids went through the usual ups and downs that adults experience in life. But I've also been successful, am part of a close family, am proud of the bond I have with my brothers and have no regrets about how we contributed to our parents' physical and emotional care in their final years. All these events in my life have created multiple emotions, both positive and negative. I like to think that these emotions can be recycled as compost to enrich my future life.

Late in 2019, I spent time in Queensland and often paddled in the surf. I would close my eyes and feel the waves come in, feel the water wash around my legs and pull back while my feet were held firmly in the wet sand. Just like recycling my feelings into compost on dry land, this was a similar representation. The surf came in and gathered the water that had been waves. I didn't need the water from those waves any longer. The tide took what I didn't need out to sea and reshaped it into a beautiful wave that came back to give me happiness.

Be inspired by Maggie.

Maggie, a young woman now in her early 30s, transitioned at 9 years old from being a child to a carer for her mum who had several chronic physical and mental health issues. She says that that period of her life set foundations for her future. In her early 20s, she became pregnant. Her mantra was, 'I know I can depend on me; I have everything I need to get through it.' I love her approach to being adaptable. Looking back now, she says, 'What I wanted for the baby was better than what I wanted for me, and I became the best version of myself – if I wanted it for him, then I needed to grow me too. We needed to grow together.'

Her curiosity is high, and she has progressively worked through various jobs and studies exploring her interests. She is curious in the workplace, always seeking to learn, testing her ideas with others, bouncing back when she needs to and challenging the status quo. Maggie is an inspiration to others who want affirmation that using adaptability, curiosity, resilience, and a growth mindset is worth it.

Personal project 16: List your catalyst moments and what you've learned

Write a list of your catalyst moments over the last year or five years or six months – whatever is relevant for you. The point is to realise what you have experienced and what you have learned. Your learnings are gold. Write them down, put the list somewhere safe. When you feel that you need a little bit of extra encouragement, please read it, and be reassured that you have everything you need.

Curiosity, adaptability, and resilience can all be learned; the only barrier is if you are unwilling to learn or if your courage fails you. This suggestion might help you when you are trying to be more adaptable, curious and resilient: when you replace 'Why is this happening to me?' with 'What is this trying to teach me?', everything shifts.

Think about this: when a child is learning to walk and falls repeatedly, maybe fifty times in a day, they don't think to themselves, 'Maybe this isn't for me.' They are curious about how they can make those little legs work. They adapt their gait as their strength and balance develop, and they try again and again and again.

You are nearly there – nearly unstoppable

CHAPTER NINE

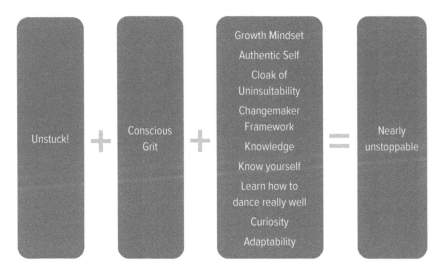

Live life 'like a boss'

Tell me, what is it you plan to do with your
one wild and precious life?

— Mary Oliver

What does 'like a boss' mean?

To do something 'like a boss' is to do it with stylish confidence or authority. This can be applied tongue in cheek even to fairly mundane tasks. (www.dictionary.com)

We all need to live like a boss when we are living life. You might be a member of a community group, the mum or dad who coaches the under-8 soccer team, the newest member of the community choir, a member of a large or small family, an employee in a workplace or the person who organises or works at the sausage sizzle on Saturdays outside the local hardware store. You might be a person who needs to make a big decision.

In this chapter, I'll share with you some of the useful skills I've learned over many years. These skills will help you to live 'like a boss' in any area of your life. After all, who doesn't want to live life or make decisions with 'stylish confidence'?

It's one thing to know about human instincts, cognitive bias, limiting beliefs, unconscious and conscious grit, and use that in your relationships and problem-solving. But when you live life like a boss, you use both management and leadership skills. In the context of this book, 'managing' others includes using both management and leadership skills to manage up, down and sideways. It also means managing yourself. These spheres form my Managing SUDS Model©.

While the words management and leadership are usually thought of in relation to the workplace, I'm applying them to all areas of life.

The four spheres of 'live life like a boss' make up my Managing SUDS Model© (Self, Up, Down, Sideways).

Managing SUDS©

Here's a scenario that shows how these four spheres connect in a workplace example.

Meet Greg.

Greg is a frontline supervisor with five members in his team. His manager, Cath, has supported his extensive professional development. Greg got excellent feedback from his team about his performance as their leader. He supported just-in-time learning, gave constructive feedback where mistakes occurred, and encouraged time for reflection. He took a planned approach to do things in a different way when team members recognised opportunities for improvement. He made sure that birthdays and work anniversaries were recognised and introduced a team member of the month award. Greg did brilliantly at **managing down**.

Greg's manager, Cath, left and was replaced by someone with a completely different management style. Allan, the new manager, emphasised deadlines, appeared not to trust Greg's way of working, had unusual explanations about external impacts on performance and said he didn't believe in soft skills, just outcomes. He only wanted to see Greg for thirty minutes every fortnight. Because Greg found the conversations uncomfortable, he didn't suggest a more suitable catch-up routine. He forgot about the importance of **managing up** and started to see his efforts as pointless. Before Allan became his boss, he could see opportunities for innovation with the other team leaders, but now he withdrew and didn't participate fully in meetings. His relationships with his peers began to decline. They saw him as isolated and hard to engage in conversations. He forgot about **managing sideways**.

He started to compare himself with other team leaders and saw himself as lacking, and the others as successful. The team could see the difference in Greg and how the changes were impacting on them. He worked long hours doing low-level busy work. Keeping busy was his way of convincing himself that he was doing a good job. But now he hates going to work. He's lost his motivation. He doesn't know how to change what's happening to him, and he doesn't understand why it's happening to him. He has forgotten to **manage himself**.

Here's an example that shows how the spheres will help in everyday life at home. Note that each of the actors has different definitions of who to manage in the sideways, up and down spheres.

Sam and Alex have three children. They both work full time, and the children are in high school and participate in after-school activities. They also support Alex's parents, who have early stage dementia and are living independently. Sam accepts an offer to work overseas for six months. Alex supports this decision. They both realise that challenges will arise. Each of them has a perspective and specific responsibilities related to the current situation. That perspective and those responsibilities influence how they manage sideways, up, down and self.

The table below shows how Sam will manage the kids thinking of them 'down'; Alex will manage them 'sideways'. This example demonstrates the value of this model. It provides a flexible framework and enables perspective to guide behaviours and actions.

	Sam's focus:	Alex's focus:
Manage sideways	Colleagues in the new workplace Relationship with Alex	Kids at home with Alex Colleagues Relationship with Sam
Manage up	Boss in the new workplace	The support agencies who can help the parents Alex's boss
Manage down	Kids at home with Alex New direct reports in the workplace	Alex's parents are becoming less able to make their own decisions

Managing self

You will have noticed a common theme in this book. You. You are important. You have the power to create and change outcomes. You can overcome your limiting beliefs. Yes, you.

In addition to the limiting beliefs that we talked about in Chapter Two, there is another form of limiting belief that manifests as imposter syndrome.

If you have imposter syndrome you are convinced that you're not as good or intelligent or talented as you may seem. You are convinced that your achievements have happened because of luck or you were in the right place at the right time. Having imposter syndrome is often accompanied by a deep-seated fear that one day somebody will uncover the fact that you're a fraud. You might have imposter syndrome to a lesser or greater extent if you feel failure and shame when:

- you are struggling to master knowledge or concepts or meet deadlines. This might happen when you start a new job, or a new boss has different expectations. Maybe you have achieved to a high level all your life – and then you become a parent. New mums and dads often struggle with the demands of parenthood

- you get 99 out of 100 and see that minor flaw to be a huge problem
- you are in a situation where you don't know everything; you like to be the one with all the knowledge and expertise.
- you need help to figure something out, but your real preference is to do it all and do it alone
- you take pride in taking on multiple roles and a level of being busy that is not sustainable and then can't manage all roles to a ridiculously high level.

Feeling failure and shame is not a good place to be, so if that's you, think about whether you have imposter syndrome. If so, here are some things you can do to mitigate the effects:

- Recognise that it is happening.
- Rewrite your mental programs from 'I need to know everything' to 'I don't need to know everything, and I'll find out more as I go along.'
- Talk about your feelings of failure and shame – you'll be surprised how many of us have these feelings all or some of the time.
- Remember that we all have moments when we feel less than 100% confident. Reframe your thinking to 'Just because I feel useless right now, doesn't mean I am useless.'
- Reframe failure or mistakes as learning opportunities.
- Be kind to yourself – we all make mistakes.

- Seek support — don't try to deal with this alone. Even a laugh with your hairdresser can put your feelings into perspective.
- Keep focused on your overall aims and goals.
- Celebrate evidence of progress and success, even if it is small.

All of these tips will be effective when you are in the conscious grit zone, and you have a growth mindset. It's all connected. Grit, growth mindset, curiosity, adaptability and courage!

You might not be able to identify that any of these descriptions apply to you. This could be for a couple of reasons. Firstly, you may not have imposter syndrome. Secondly, you may have it, but don't recognise it. You could use your courage to ask a trusted friend or mentor if they see any of these things in you.

Mentoring can be awesome — or not so awesome

The concept of mentorship is a powerful one for managing self. But mentorship doesn't always work.

I participated in a mentoring program as a mentor some years ago. The process of connecting the mentors and the mentees was uncomfortable and clunky. It didn't bode well for good outcomes. All the mentors spoke about what they could offer. Then, over coffee, the mentees approached the mentors they were attracted to and asked them to be their mentor.

There was no opportunity to find out from the mentee what they needed from a mentoring relationship. There was no opportunity to say no. Sadly, there was an unspoken sense that if you had hierarchy and status, you were a more valuable commodity as a mentor.

I walked out of the room that day with three mentees. This was unsustainable, and I know that I wasn't the best choice for any of them.

Mentors are most effective when mentors and mentees find each other through an organic process; without a doubt, that is what has worked for me as a mentor and a mentee. The relationship may last for several years, or it may evolve to a supportive friendship. The relationship may be useful for just a few weeks or months. It may be targeted to a particular issue, developmental need or time and place. There are no rights or wrongs. While mentors are often associated with the workplace or sporting environments, a mentor can be valuable in other areas of your life, such as when:

- you are getting married, and you don't want to cave in to the pressure of others about arrangements
- you need to navigate the National Disability Insurance Scheme for a family member
- you've got the puppy you have always wanted and it's barking frequently, chewing your furniture and harassing your visitors
- you've built a house, and you don't know where to start with a garden
- you know your art is good but feel like giving up as you can't find a market for it.

There are some guidelines for being a good mentor and a good mentee.

An effective mentor will:

- have experience and expertise that is relevant
- steer the mentee through tight spots
- care about the mentee's success
- have a growth mindset
- believe in the mentee
- gain the trust and confidence of the mentee.

An effective mentee will:

- be motivated to act on the knowledge they have received
- commit time to make the mentoring worthwhile
- have a growth mindset
- be honest
- communicate that they understand what the mentor is teaching them and how they are applying it.

You might decide that you need some support. It could be a mentor that you need.

There is also great value in having a personal coach. It will cost you – they vary in price – but it can be worthwhile. The main predictor of whether you get value from the investment is the connection between you and the coach. You may need to shop around. And the next predictor of value is your commitment to follow up with actions or make changes where that needs to happen. If you meet somebody and don't connect with that person, then you know that is not your coach. Keep looking.

Managing up

A wise man once said to me, 'Everyone has a master, Gail.' I was arguing with him about why he'd made a particular decision! He was giving me a strong hint that he disagreed with the decision he needed to implement.

Even when you live life 'like a boss', you will also have a boss. That boss will have a job to do, outcomes they're trying to achieve, and they will also have a boss. Your job is to manage up – to develop a complementary way of working so that outcomes can be achieved.

You will need to be in the zone of conscious grit to be able to do this. It won't all be smooth sailing.

You'll need to find out your manager's style, values, and needs in terms of information updates and communication preferences. It's the same whether you are in the workplace or managing the local footy team that plays in the regional roster.

You need to be seen as capable, competent, able to work in a team and have a genuine desire to advance the interests of the business, the team or the sport overall.

If you do manage up, you will develop a relationship with those above you that will lead to harmony, productivity and a sense of satisfaction that you have contributed to the outcomes of the business or the team. You will also have better information flow that you can then use with your team to help them perform well.

You will need to find out which matters you need to brief upwards and which you can deal with yourself. Knowing what to brief up or manage independently is one of the areas that tests relationships.

Even the most robust risk assessment, planning and treatment programs will come unstuck if there is no clear understanding of who needs to know what and when.

The best advice I can give here is to take a 'no surprises approach'. That is, don't ever assume that those above you didn't need to know. And early advice is always best as well.

Meet Joe.

Joe is the CEO of a service that supports people with disabilities. Board directors say they only want to be involved in strategic matters. They have made it clear that operations are Joe's domain. On a visit to a client, one of the support workers has a car accident. There are no injuries to the worker, the car has damage that can be fixed, but it will be off the road for a few weeks. The accident was witnessed by one of the Board directors. Joe doesn't tell the Board this has happened. He makes the judgement that it's an operational matter.

The Board Chair is told about the accident by the director who saw it. He is angry with Joe for not telling him. Joe says it's an operational matter. The Board Chair says it's a matter of risk and finances and that he and the Board should have been told about it. He wants to know what else Joe is not telling him. Joe could have 'managed up' by advising the Board of the accident and consequences while making it clear that no action was needed on their part.

Managing up doesn't happen in isolation of managing sideways, self and down.

Meet Tess. Her 8-year-old child is bullied at school.

Tess needs to manage up with the teacher, school principal and school psychologist. These are the people that are influential in making changes to the school structure where the bullying is happening. Tess needs to manage sideways. She should get support from the other parents at the school and secure services to support her and her child, such as counselling services. In this context, Tess might be tempted to manage down inappropriately. She must treat the perpetrators of the bullying – and their parents – in a way that doesn't exacerbate the situation. To do all of this in a measured and effective way, Tess will need to manage herself. She will need to recognise that emotion before reason will likely prevail but that acting out of emotion will not elicit an appropriate response.

Those who you are managing up might need help

This is a tricky topic from another perspective, particularly in the workplace. Just because your boss is in the role they are in, they may not be doing the role well.

One way to deal with this is to collaborate with your colleagues and operate from the zone of conscious grit using good intent and a spirit of advancing the common good.

Meet a strong executive team.

This team decided that they needed to 'manage up' so that they could maximise the time they spent at meetings and get clarification around decisions. They decided that five actions would meet their needs:

- Distribute meeting papers ahead of the meeting.

- Use a shared electronic platform for the papers.
- Set a realistic agenda.
- Distribute action points (not minutes) within twenty-four hours of the meeting.
- Update feedback from previous actions at the start of each meeting.

They agreed that they would put the matter on the agenda with one of their names against it. They would support the person who spoke to the agenda item and provide a rationale against the pushback they knew they would get. They persisted with their requests, and their boss finally agreed. Future meetings were more productive, targeted and action-focused. The new way of working helped them all do their jobs. They collectively managed up.

Be respectful of individuality

The person you are managing up to may operate in a completely different way to you. Neither is right or wrong. They are just different modes. You may need to be creative in the interests of managing up effectively.

Meet Helen.

At the interview, Helen noticed that Veronica, her boss to be, was quiet.

Helen knew from Veronica's reputation that she had excellent technical skills. Helen noticed quickly that Veronica was not strong in people management and communication skills.

By week three, Helen hadn't had an induction, she had many questions for Veronica, and no opportunities to catch up or meet had been scheduled. Helen spoke to Veronica's EA, who explained that Veronica doesn't generally meet with direct reports individually — contact would be at monthly team meetings. As it turns out, Veronica is a morning person, introverted and shy. Helen used conscious grit, authenticity, mindset and curiosity to find a way to develop a relationship with Veronica and get the information she needed. It involved delivering a chai latte to Veronica's office around 8 am every Thursday, for a forty-five minute chat.

Personal project 17: Private thinking

When values or behavioural styles clash, there will be trouble unless the clash is mitigated. For example:

- Melanie likes face-to-face meetings. Her boss likes quick phone calls between 9 and 9.30 in the morning. Melanie is likely to be doing the school run at that time. How can that be managed?
- Tom values inclusion. His boss regularly leaves people out of meeting invitations. How could Tom manage that?
- Sarah's boss likes to make the final decision at meetings. Sarah is very committed to a consensus approach. How can Sarah manage that?

Here's an exercise for you.

Analyse your boss's behaviour and values. Now write down yours. Compare the lists. This personal project is not about who is right and who is wrong. It is about identifying where there is common ground and where there are gaping voids. These gaps do happen.

Some matters, or gaps, will be more critical than others. Some will be more urgent than others. You will be able to put some to the bottom of the list or discard them. Where there is a misalignment that you want to sort out, think about who needs to move their position. It might be you, in part or in full.

Use this grid to help you sort out your ideas.

I want to change it - I need help to deal with this	I have the skills and tools to influence this
I'm not sure I can move on this one	I need to accept this

You can also do this exercise to help you sort out your thinking if you are in conflict with a family member – or want to avoid getting into conflict.

Here is a simple example: a well-meaning family member drops in all the time with treats for the 4- and 8-year-old children.

I want to change it – I need help	**I have the skills and tools to influence this**
I feel intimidated by their loud voice and the way they seem to think that our home is theirs	I can tell them why I don't want them to bring sugary treats at bedtime and suggest other things
I'm not sure I can move on this one	**I can accept this**
Bringing the sugary treats at bedtime	Dropping in without notice

Managing down

I admit this concept sounds awful. Even disrespectful. But this sphere is a useful way to approach and manage some relationships and interactions. If we 'managed down' in a literal way, we would lose sight of the potential of others. The concept of 'down' seems to imply weakness and lacking in value. This is most definitely not what I mean. Every one of us has life experiences, current and past circumstances, attitudes, characteristics, and behavioural styles that they bring to the community, clubs, family and workplace every day, because that's who they are.

There is value in finding out what people who you may have placed in the managing down sphere do in their spare time, what their hobbies are, and what their 'hidden' skills are. Then create opportunities to use those skills.

I recall discovering a team member who would spend the entire weekend caring for their high-needs disabled sibling to give their parents a break. In another section of this organisation were an experienced small plane pilot and an award-winning dog breeder. There was a person who ran a sporting competition on the weekends and another who regularly performed as an actor and singer.

The skills that these five people had were extraordinary. When you find these hidden skills in people, give them more opportunities to contribute to the workplace. They'll be happier, the community, family, club or workplace will benefit, and you will have affirmed their fantastic skill set. For example, the actor and singer became our regular 'Master of Ceremonies' for very large events and was brilliant at it.

One of the challenges we face as we age is taking on the mantle of being carer or guardian for older members in the family.

The concept of managing down became very relevant to me when my parents became ill. Dad was not doing well. He was putting confidence before realism, not wanting to recognise how poorly mum was. I needed to manage that situation. I used my 'stylish confidence' to manage down when dealing with my parents.

I know many people who are or have been in this situation. It is not a comfortable place to be. It's a strange feeling to be managing the smallest details of the lives of the people you spent years looking up to. When you find a framework to do this in, it helps. For me, it was respectfully managing down.

One way of thinking about managing down means managing those people who report to you and those in your area, division or department.

When you are seen as the boss by others, relationships will change. I know you think that won't happen. But it will.

You say, 'It will all be okay; these people were my friends; they encouraged me to apply. We even had a celebratory afternoon tea when it was announced that I had won the role.'

I say, 'Enjoy the celebratory afternoon tea and the happiness of achieving a career goal. Then add a dose of reality.'

Add in emotion before reason, confidence before realism, loss aversion, cognitive biases and your reaction to pressures from above you. Add in any number of external changes – these could be political, legal, technological, client-based, environmental. The strengths and weaknesses of the people you are now managing become more evident to you. The workplace behavioural styles that were once endearing are now annoying. You may even see their style as obstructive and disruptive. Now it's your responsibility to deal with it. The ability to manage down needs to be in your tool kit.

Meet Jane and Christine.

Jane became a team leader after several attempts at applying for the role. She had aspired to it for several years. Jane had good technical skills and was a vibrant, well-liked personality in the team. She loved being the person who organised the social events and spent time with her workmates outside of working hours. Jane always seemed to be able to find out what was happening in other areas of the organisation. She was 'networked' and liked being able to keep others informed. Jane had sound leadership skills. She was a volunteer firefighter.

Fortunately, Jane had a mentor who helped her understand that one of her first tasks as the new boss was to set boundaries. This was essential for her success in the role.

Jane explained to her team members that in her new role, she would have access to information that she would not be able to share with them. She committed to being visible, and to participate in social events outside work hours where she was able to. She could not allow alcohol into the workplace drinks at 5 pm Friday.

This set her up well for managing the team. Setting boundaries does not prevent others from acting according to their hard-wired instincts (putting emotion before reason, for example). Still, it does provide a safety net when there are conflicts or undercurrents in the workplace.

This happened.

Christine had acted in the team leader role before and had not been appointed for the permanent role. She was disappointed in the outcome. Her disappointment showed in her behaviour. She 'bagged' Jane, for her change of position around the long-standing custom of having alcoholic drinks after work. She gossiped with others about Jane's 'withholding of information' that was going to affect the team.

With support from her mentor, Jane had a challenging conversation with the emotional Christine and reminded her about the boundaries that she had set – upfront, noticeably clear, and sensible. Christine composed herself enough to apologise. Their relationship was never the same, but they were able to have a constructive and productive team leader/team member relationship.

A key to managing down successfully is to 'walk the talk'. Not doing so is a sure way to lose your supporters and your team will disengage.

Meet Ian.

Ian had just started as an area manager. In week one, he got an opportunity to talk to his team. Amongst other things, he spoke about his values, one of which was inclusion. Six months later, Ian appointed a person who was visually impaired. Ian invested in technology and the physical environment to support the new person in their role. He was commended for this.

However, Ian was inconsistent about his claimed value of inclusion. He rarely invited others to contribute. He issued communiques each fortnight in a one-way flow of communication. Only some staff were invited to the annual planning day. His team members noticed this. They talked amongst themselves, particularly around the water cooler.

Over the next few months, Ian's staff only notice him when he is not including others. They become increasingly disengaged. Deadlines slip. Unfortunately, no one in the group dares to raise the matter with him. This continues until the staff start to leave. Ian is so focused on managing himself (think contest and display) that he has missed all the signs that his team need him. The drop in performance is noticed, and eventually, he is replaced. There were no winners in this scenario.

Ian didn't have a mentor. If he had, his mentor could have helped Ian match his values to his behaviours and this gap may have been identified and resolved early on.

Personal project 18: Get your walking shoes on

Relationships are the foundation of success. One of the ways that I have found success in 'managing down' is getting out and talking to staff as they go about their roles.

If this is a new approach in the workplace, I guarantee you will get some suspicious looks. You may even be asked, 'What are you here for?' My natural curiosity served me well in these activities. I am genuinely interested in what people are doing, how they are doing it, and how they feel about the workplace – the good and the bad. I'm also interested in how long they've been employees and how the role has changed over time.

You will need to judge if you should appear without notice; consider the culture and any overt or covert messaging you have received.

However, it is probably safer to let them know you are coming, and you are going to walk around and have some informal chats. They don't need to prepare. Ask them to tell you if there are areas where it will be too busy to go on that day. Ask about any PPE considerations you might need.

These are the kinds of questions I use. Put your spin on them — make it a conversation, not an interview, and use your intuition. If you find that you are asking questions of the trainee who only started three weeks ago and is nervous, adapt and focus on welcoming them to the organisation.

Out and about questions:

- What does your role entail?
- What makes you happy at work?
- What help do you need?
- What resources do you need over and above what you have now?
- If you could change anything, what would it be?
- Are the resources we've given you the right ones to do the job?
- Are they there when you need them?
- Are there ways we can improve the workplace?
- Do you have time to reflect and learn from the wins and the challenges of your everyday work?

In using this approach, I've discovered and then resolved many issues that were important to employees. There were many reasons why they hadn't been addressed. My list includes a leaking roof, damaged and outdated mobile phones, headsets that were held together with Blu Tack, and single screens being used for complex all-day work on databases. I've found multiple desks crammed into an office space with little regard for work health and safety. I've seen some departments expanding into the physical space of others, with no regard for impact on operations. I've heard about reasonable requests, for learning and development, being denied with inefficient process, flawed rationale and little communication.

Six rules apply to ensure that this is an effective and positive exercise.

Rule one – follow up what you have said you will fix.

Rule two – remember to communicate with anyone who might not like that you are out and about. Others may see you as snooping or interfering, depending on their role in the organisation. Stay authentic and operate from the zone of conscious grit.

Rule three – deal with information or observations prudently.

Rule four – don't make promises you can't keep.

Rule five – always keep your peers and other people in the loop.

Rule six – repeat the walking around activity at intervals. You need to demonstrate that your interest is genuine and not opportunistic.

Personal project 19: Performance review

Another way to manage down in the workplace is to maximise the benefit of a performance review. I've never enjoyed or valued the standard template (often of many pages) that is required by HR departments. I prefer to have a discussion and then document what's agreed to be actioned and monitored. That, of course, is a battle you will need to have with your HR department!

The value comes from the discussion and input from both you and your staff members. I like to do an informal assessment in the form of a SWOT analysis – analysis of strengths, weaknesses, opportunities, threats – from both your perspectives.

Once you've done that, go a step further and think about what you can do to maximise their strengths, strengthen their weaknesses, optimise the opportunities, and counter the threats.

Meet Brett.

Brett has been with the organisation as a finance officer for thirty years. He can't wait for retirement. He's been a solid performer over many years; he's a man of few words but when he speaks, he is funny. His team leader and his colleagues feel that he is just coasting along. It's a small team, but the workload is ever-increasing and everyone does need to pull their weight.

Here's an analysis for Brett:

Strengths	Weaknesses
Funny, sense of humour	Doesn't speak up in meetings
Well liked	Puts emotion before reason
Gets things done on time	
Opportunities	**Threats**
Update his knowledge of methods	Will likely retire in twelve months
Find ways to use his experience	Corporate knowledge will be lost

Use the information from Chapter Six to add depth to your analysis:

- Does he have limiting beliefs? Does he think he has limiting beliefs?
- What human instincts is he using? What human instincts does he think he's using? For example, emotion before reason, confidence before realism.
- How are his responses to events influencing outcomes?

Brett's plan will:

- maximise his strengths by praising him, and encourage him to maintain timeliness and to coach others in the team to develop these strengths
- strengthen weaknesses by letting him know that you would like him to prepare a paper for a meeting and present it at the meeting
- optimise opportunities by having him mentor other staff
- ask him to document areas of work that you don't want to lose after his retirement.

Brett will feel valued, included, rewarded, stretched and affirmed. He will be more engaged in the workplace. Others will benefit from him sharing his wisdom, and the organisation won't lose his corporate knowledge.

Here's an example that doesn't relate to the workplace. It's a 'performance review' of a different kind. Allie's best friend Sarah has a 6-year-old with challenging behaviours. Allie wants to help Sarah and does a simple SWOT analysis to start with.

Sarah's strengths are that she is loving, caring, has housing and financial stability. Is a good person and wouldn't want to hurt or harm her child. Wants to find a way to help her child regulate her behaviour.	Sarah's weaknesses include that she is tired, indulges the child with treats to coerce positive behaviour, has low literacy.
Sarah has the opportunity to use the abundant non-written resources available.	A threat to the situation is that Sarah is so frustrated that she is now locking the child in her room as punishment, making the problem worse.

Having written this down, it's obvious to Allie that she could help Sarah by:

- acknowledging Sarah's strengths and building her confidence
- helping Sarah see that finding a way to help her child regulate her behaviour is possible
- go with her to a child development/behaviour expert for a face-to-face chat
- show her videos about children's development, behaviour and appropriate behaviour management.

You are not everyone's cup of tea

One lesson I have learned in 'managing down' is that other people will push back. This happens in our personal and professional lives. You might remember that when I was in the zone of conscious grit, I experienced pushback from some family members. And I've experienced it in the workplace as well.

The people that you are managing will have a variety of feelings and opinions about you. The reality is that none of us is everybody's cup of tea. Workplace dynamics play a part as well. You might have displaced somebody that was well loved and respected. You may now be the boss of someone who had acted in the role several times and saw the role as theirs.

I also know that the culture – the way we do things around here – is not something that you can change quickly or by yourself. People often feel suspicious about what you might be up to when you are trying to 'manage down'. If they have been 'burned' by a boss previously, you will have to work hard to build trust.

I remember in one of my walks around, an employee challenged me about my background. He didn't know about my experience or qualifications. He just knew that I was 'in his patch'. It was also unusual behaviour for a boss to be out and about in that workplace. I told him about my background and qualifications, some interesting things I had done in my career, and my values. I maintained a conversational tone and asked him about his experiences and qualifications, and his career highlights to date. His body language, facial expressions and tone changed dramatically, and for the better. Be ready, as something similar might happen to you.

It's usual for a new boss to set the tone with people who report to them, or generally in their work unit, about 'how we do things around here'. This includes setting expectations.

Meet Melanie and Dean.

In her first month in her role as a frontline supervisor, Melanie heard lots of excuses from her direct report Dean about why he couldn't complete tasks:

- I didn't have time.
- My colleague didn't give me the information I needed.
- I have too many things on my list, and they are all critical.

Melanie's initial way of dealing with this was to say with gritted teeth, 'Okay,' and 'I'll take care of it.' This was not sustainable for Melanie and not a constructive way to deal with Dean. He wasn't learning and wasn't stretching himself. He wasn't doing his job. After mentoring, Melanie took a different approach. She expressed disappointment to Dean that the task wasn't done, got curious, and asked more questions about the reasons it wasn't done. She set firm expectations about future deadlines and the steps Dean needed to take if it looked like he couldn't get the task done. Melanie also engaged Dean in a discussion about how he could adapt the tasks to take less time. Melanie used the traits of curiosity, adaptability, and growth mindset (as discussed earlier in the book) to steer Dean's performance as she needed it to be. It worked.

Managing sideways

Managing sideways may seem like a strange concept. For some, it may already be occurring but in an ad hoc way without any deliberate thought put into it.

Let's say you are moving house. There are lots of jobs to be done. You could choose to be directive and take the position of 'top dog'. This might work, or you might put people offside and end up having to repair relationships. Others involved might decide they are not going to help you in the future because of the way you have handled it. Or you could take a sideways approach and engage everyone involved in a collaborative approach. The job will get done, relationships are more likely to be intact, and you can ask the same people again for help in the future.

In workplaces, there will always be people that we need to work with. As well as those above you, you need to work with your colleagues and peers, and you may have direct reports. There will be tension. Sometimes it will be palpable. At other times it will be subliminal. Tension can arise when peers and colleagues disagree on an approach, or you might be competing for promotion. Levels of commitment to the organisation will also be variable. All of this needs to be managed. And whilst your peers are being managed by you, you will be being managed by them. Sound complicated? It is.

I don't think that hierarchical management structures bring out the best in organisations and people. In short, innovation gets stifled, acting is often slow, and layers of unnecessary decision-making cause frustration for clients, customers and staff. Managing sideways is a way to break out of hierarchical management structures. It will help you bridge the inevitable gaps between your department and other departments.

As a member of an executive or management team – or any group – you need to manage your relationships with others, or you will be at an immediate disadvantage. We know from the work on hard-wired human instincts that constructive gossip is a good thing.

You've probably been involved in this without realising. Opportunities like having the water cooler conversations in the office, the chat over a coffee, the school car park chats at pick-up and drop-off times ensure you are in the loop and help you feel like an active part of a group. How many of us have experienced the teenager who communicates with grunts and facial expressions until you get them in the car on your own and you then have a good talk. Being in the car is a great opportunity for constructive gossip.

There are other benefits for you. You can educate other managers about your team's activities and needs by strategically sharing updates with them.

You get to know other bosses. When you know their strengths, weaknesses, aspirations and experiences, you can approach the right person at the right time to help you achieve your outcomes. In this way, you can also help them achieve their results.

Meet Monica and Paul.

Monica had been at a meeting and heard one of the other bosses, Paul, mention an organisational problem impacting on customer service. She had also experienced this problem. Monica went to Paul after the meeting and said she had a similar problem and some ideas for additional staff training. She asked him if her ideas might solve the problem from his perspective. He thought so, and they set about working together to solve the problem. Before they worked together, they both had the problem, and neither was inspired to fix it. Then they were both inspired to work together, and the problem was solved.

Monica and Paul 'joined the dots'. An unintended benefit was that Monica's team and Paul's team trained together, built relationships, and have a new system for sharing staff resources during peaks and troughs in the workflow.

Collaboration is essential when you're thinking about managing sideways. Collaboration has a simple definition, but sometimes people overcomplicate it. It's two or more people working together towards a shared goal or goals. That's all.

You might be one of ten team leaders or frontline supervisors. You might all have the same role description. As a group, you are responsible for the outcomes of the organisation. Or you might be a middle or senior manager responsible for a particular aspect of the organisation. Let's say you are accountable for quality. Other equivalent managers are responsible for policy, business development and human resources. As a group, you are responsible for the systems and processes that will ensure the success of the business. You all have strengths, so exploit them. It's too tempting to see another section as 'the enemy'.

In the context of collaborating when in the zone of conscious grit, there are some simple tips:

- Be available and willing to help others with their problems. Persist with the issue until the person you are collaborating with says, 'Thanks – I've got it now.'
- Be determined to give feedback in the way that's requested (verbal or writing) and meet your timelines to do so.
- Be tenacious in asking for feedback from your boss, peers, your team. This shows that you value their expertise.
- Share useful knowledge, research or intel.
- Be determined to develop relationships.
- Share credit – your collaboration partner will share the credit with you in the future.

- Dare to take the blame. If you make a mistake, own it.

Beware – ego can get in the way

Ego can get in the way. If you are concerned that others will get the credit for the achievement of outcomes, or others may scoop up your ideas, or that you won't be recognised for effort, you might struggle with this concept of managing sideways.

Trust me when I say that it is gratifying to see people come together to work on a project or a task. I love to see the dynamics as someone emerges as a leader.

I also love to see members encourage others when a new team is forming. I love to hear 'Okay,' and 'I'll give that a go,' and 'I'll give you a hand.' Or 'Have you thought of doing it another way?' or 'Have you read the latest research?'

Leadership coach Angela Kambouris, in a *Leaders in Heels*[29] article, is emphatic:

> *De-emphasising where an idea comes from and moving from the 'I' to the 'we', creates an environment where there is no room for prima donnas. A 'we' leader will solicit ideas from all levels, encouraging people who experiment with different ideas and championing unsuccessful efforts. A phenomenal leader thrives*

---

29   https://leadersinheels.com/category/career/self-development/page/5/

from the accomplishment of the team and strives for the greater good of the organisation.

The team collaboration process – forming, storming, norming and performing

When you manage sideways, an organic process happens. Teams of people will come together for short or long periods to share knowledge, to problem-solve, make improvements, share resources and celebrate success. Those teams won't show up on the organisational structure as a team.

However, they are a team. As with all groups, the team will progress through processes of forming, storming, norming and finally performing. These processes might happen quickly or slowly. It is essential to recognise that they **will** happen and not be discouraged if you don't get the outcome you want straight away.

Dr Bruce Tuckman[30], a psychology professor, proposed the form, storm, norm and perform model in the 1960s. In the context of managing sideways, you can self-nominate as the leader, identify the problem and who needs to be involved in the collaboration.

This is how the concepts of forming, storming, norming, performing and managing sideways align.

Forming. This is often the easy bit. As the leader of the 'managing sideways' process, you tell those who you want to be involved in sorting out the problem to bring their skills, knowledge and

---

30   https://en.wikipedia.org/wiki/Tuckman%27s_stages_of_group_development

experience to the table. I've always found coffee and food helps as well!

Storming. Different views and perspectives emerge, personalities become apparent, and egos may appear. Communicating well is vital at this stage. And be ready for conflict. You will also see positive intent. Hang in there. It's only a stage.

Norming. A common understanding emerges. If storming has been allowed to happen AND managed well, norming will 'just happen'. The team will start to develop trust in and respect for each other (maybe not acceptance) and their different perspectives.

Performing. The focus is on the problem to be solved or the matter at hand. There might still be challenges, but positive intent prevails, and you will get an outcome.

If someone leaves the group, or something changes in the environment, you can always go back to one of the other stages.

Meet Andrew.

Andrew leads a team. He is struggling to understand conflicting advice being given to his team. Varied information is coming from the quality and improvement team, the business development team and the audit team. Each of the leaders of these areas is a peer, according to the organisational structure. He asks them to meet with him so they can find the best way forward. The first meeting has all the features of 'storming'. Everyone wants to have their say and to put their definitive position. At the second meeting, their views are not as binary and comments like 'I hear what you are saying,' and 'What about if we thought about it this way?' are heard.

At the third meeting, members are talking about the fact that this has been a beneficial collaborative discussion. And that maybe they could use it to resolve similar issues where there is conflicting advice.

And then there is a result. There is some give and take, some understanding, some standing ground around regulatory aspects. But there is a result. The group has performed. There is an agreement to amend and align processes and develop more straightforward templates.

Managing sideways vs managing down

In line with the hard-wiring of humans and the tendency for us to enjoy hierarchy and status, it's often tempting to manage down. Changing the way you respond from 'managing down' to 'managing sideways' will often give you a different outcome.

Meet a marketing team.

Twenty people use the fridge in the staff room. The take-away shop down the road got burnt down. Everyone is bringing their lunch and snacks to work. The fridge is overflowing. There are the usual signs on the wall instructing everyone to clear out their food at the end of the week. No one does. One Friday, Suzanne has a meltdown about the fridge. She blames everyone, throws all the food into the sink and sets about cleaning the refrigerator.

Meanwhile, the deadline for the critical task Suzanne is working on for a client passes. She is now in trouble with the team leader.

If you apply the 'sideways' approach in this situation, this is how it might look. The team leader could get a few people involved in solving the problem. They could ask for a couple of staff volunteers and facilitate a discussion with them, the cleaner, the person whose job it is to keep the kitchen tidy and the organiser of the social club (who has stored all the soft drink in the fridge and is taking up space). By using this approach, the core problem is identified, and agreement for resolution is reached through consensus. Further, the plan for the future is likely to be sustained. Everyone knows the problem, the solution and their role.

If a 'down' approach is applied, the team leader might simply create a new sign for the wall and send an email around telling everyone to keep the kitchen clean. This approach won't contribute to a positive outcome. Fifty per cent of the staff will delete the email without reading, the sign will have no effect, and Suzanne will continue to be frustrated. The problem will continue.

CHAPTER TEN

Conscious grit can be overdone

Tomorrow is the most important thing in life. Comes into us at midnight very clean. It's perfect when it arrives and it puts itself in our hands. It hopes we've learned something from yesterday.

— John Wayne

Overdone conscious grit

When you're in the zone of conscious grit there'll be momentum; you'll be pushing forward, planning, getting others involved in your journey and showing heaps of courage. Sometimes your pace will be too fast and your commitment too deep. Your judgements can start to be a little off kilter. It's important to calibrate your efforts in the zone of conscious grit to the level that will serve you well.

Often when things are overdone, there is a negative consequence. A flippant example is that you ask for your steak to be medium-rare and it comes back medium-well. That's disappointing for you, and the chef or waitress may hear about it!

Another example comes from a behaviour that many of us have engaged in during the COVID-19 pandemic: baking. It was a welcome change in our household until I stacked on some kilos and my husband suffered gout from the sugar. They were signs that I'd overdone baking yummy, sweet things.

There are of course other examples that aren't flippant. Think about a toddler. Determined, tenacious, persistent and resilient in their exploration of the world. Without doubt they are displaying 'big C' Courage. And they may have a plan and a future focus. Sadly, sometimes that conscious grit gets them into big trouble. It is overdone in comparison to their developmental ability. They may end up crossing the road or climbing a pool fence to retrieve a ball.

Strengths can backfire despite good intentions. People may give you a clue that you are on the border of overdoing things. I remember one of my team saying to me years ago, 'Gail, there is a certain look you get in your eye sometimes and I know that you are just not ever going to give up!' I remember from her tone that this was not a compliment!

Overdone strengths have the potential to trigger conflict, damage relationships and derail productivity. You may recognise these overdone strengths:

- the person who comes across as ruthless when they are just overdoing ambition
- the person who overdoes being helpful and is seen as smothering

- the person who is methodical but comes across as rigid and inflexible
- the person who's open to change and is seen as inconsistent.

The common factor in all of these examples is that the desire to be unstoppable overrides your rational brain.

How to know if conscious grit is being overdone

Conscious grit	Signs that conscious grit is being overdone
Tenacity	Inability to let go when it's sensible to do so. Being tenacious about everything and for all situations and contexts.
Determination	Your opinion might not always be right or give the best results. You might be so determined to press your perspective on others that you become angry.
Perseverance	Investing more and more resources over an extended period of time, but there just won't be a return.
Resilience	Bouncing back repeatedly without any reflection about the cause.
Planning	Planning to the ultimate degree in an intense way. Planning everything and not involving or considering others.
Future focus	Disregarding the practicalities of day-to-day operating.
'Big C' Courage	Risk-taking without proper assessment and management.

Meet Jenny.

Jenny has been in the zone of conscious grit for several months. Unfortunately, the business that she works for has been amalgamated with a competitor, and the amalgamation is due to take effect in two months' time.

Jenny is feeling threatened, displaced and worried about her financial future. She's had a positive relationship with her boss. However, he has been moved to another section. Communication flow about the amalgamation is minimal. Her values of respect, honesty and inclusion are challenged. In fact, her world has been rocked.

She's become angrier and more frustrated as the weeks have gone by.

She can't let go of issues and is being unreasonably tenacious in all situations and contexts. Her interactions with others are becoming uncomfortable. She is so determined to have her perspective heard that raising her voice and being obviously angry are common occurrences. She is working longer and longer hours. However, this won't fix what she is frustrated about.

She gets up every day and goes into the office. She thinks she's being resilient, but all Jenny is doing is getting out of bed and travelling to work. She is not resilient in terms of working towards long-term goals. There is nothing constructive in her future focus: she doesn't have one, so planning for it is absent.

Her heart rate often accelerates, her blood pressure rises and her rate of breathing increases. Her face is flushed as increased blood flow enters her limbs and extremities in preparation for the fight reaction.

She pays attention to nothing other than her own situation. Her team misses her guidance and support, her attention to detail, her positive tenacity and her passion for them and their work. Jenny needs to rebalance. Her body is telling her that things need to change.

Jenny's reactions can be described and explained by some simple brain science that focuses on emotions. Emotions come from the arousal of the nervous system. Millions of chemical reactions take place in the brain at any given time. Chemical reactions occur through synapses, which are parts of the nervous system. Through synapses, neurons transmit messages using neurotransmitters. Emotions are typically measured in physiological responses like those that we saw in Jenny: pounding heart, sweating, blood rushing to the face, and the release of adrenaline.

Expression is also a major part of emotions and it's associated with parts of the nervous system such as the motor cortex, the limbic system and the brain stem. The parts of the nervous system that affect emotion the most are the frontal lobes and the amygdala.

The frontal cortex is usually associated with feelings of happiness and pleasure. The amygdala is usually associated with feelings of anger, fear and sadness. The amygdala is also responsible for identifying threats to our wellbeing and then sending out an alarm. It's so effective that you've probably heard that we get 'hijacked' by the amygdala, because it influences us to act before we consider the consequences of our actions. It triggers our fight response.

Sandra is Jenny's new supervisor. Sandra doesn't know about brain science so her reaction and response to Jenny is to tell her to pull herself together and deal with it.

Jenny doesn't respond well to this. Her emotional response continues and will do so whilst the amygdala is still in alarm mode. When you think about this scenario from the perspective of brain science, some things are out of her control. However, Jenny can act to control some of her emotional responses. She can take time off, talk to someone, get some exercise, and practise meditation or mindfulness. This will encourage her rational brain to come to the fore and she will be able to manage her relationship with Sandra.

Here are twelve points that I find useful in managing relationships:

- Deliberately build trust. It is the foundation of every good relationship. When there is trust, you can be open and honest in your thoughts and actions.
- Foster the development of mutual respect. You can do this by valuing others' ideas and input. They will value yours. That leads to a mutual valuing of collective insight, creativity and wisdom.
- Take responsibility for your words and actions.
- Value inclusion and diversity; make sure all people are welcome in discussions, and all opinions are considered and factored into decision-making.
- Communicate in timely ways.
- Communicate with others taking their preferences for email, phone or face-to-face into account.
- Give and receive feedback and news: good, bad and downright ugly.
- Handle conflict with diplomacy, tact and a win-win approach.
- Nurture your ability to move on, even though it might be hard to do so.
- Collaborate, cooperate and share information, resources and opportunities.
- Be empathetic to emotional cues and perspectives.
- Want other people to have development opportunities and be successful. Show that it is important to you.

I've applied these points to the scenario that Jenny and Sandra find themselves in. Jenny is in the zone of overdone conscious grit and Sandra needs some help with relationship management.

Let's say that I've been asked to observe the relationship and interactions between Jenny and Sandra. After talking to each of them and being a quiet observer, I write to each of them. I would use the tone of being a mentor to Sandra. Here is my letter to her:

Dear Sandra

I can see you are having a tough time — you are in a difficult position managing the demands of an amalgamation process. I can also see that Jenny needs some additional support now. My advice to you is based on my relationship management tips.

Jenny is a senior and experienced manager. You could talk to Jenny in confidence. Put some boundaries around what can be shared. She will respond well.

Jenny's expertise can benefit you. Involve her in committees; her corporate knowledge will be invaluable, and she is keen to share it.

You could ask Jenny to take on the role of putting together some regular communication to staff. You would have input into the content and the final sign-off. Jenny knows the staff well and can tailor the messages so they are heard. Jenny will feel valued and will reinforce your messages to the team.

Jenny has great facilitation skills; you could convene a workshop with staff from both organisations. The workshop should focus on identifying what needs to be taken forward and not lost after amalgamation. Jenny could facilitate this workshop and report back to you with some recommendations.

You will have noticed that Jenny is having physical responses to the stress of the situation. You could give her a voucher to have a massage – or something similar. Let her know you care. You could even share your own stress. It's not easy for you either.

Finally, ask Jenny about her aspirations. Help her develop a plan to get there. Ask her to do the same with her team and let her know you welcome further discussions to hear about their needs.

Best wishes

Your Mentor

As Jenny's mentor, I would provide guidance; she needs to play her part too. Here's my letter to her:

Dear Jenny

Sandra is going to meet with you tomorrow. I want to give you some ideas about how to approach the conversation – I know you might be concerned about how it will go.

My advice to you is simple. Trust that Sandra's motivation is positive and be honest and open with her.

Sandra is also having a difficult time; ask her about her prior experience and what she likes to do outside of work.

Do some preparation before the meeting. Write down the dominant feelings that are bothering you now and be prepared to talk about them for just a few minutes in the meeting.

Take a list of the things that your team is concerned about and talk them through calmly. Put forward your solutions where you have them. Focus on the things that you know will have high impact if you can get them resolved: communication, reassurances for staff, development opportunities for you and the team.

Sandra won't be able to agree with everything you put forward – she also has a master. There may be some things she can't approve. Ask her to take those away and come back to you.

Make a list of your skills and tell her how you will contribute them to the amalgamation. Be clear with Sandra about the value of those skills and what they will bring to the project.

And finally, remember that you have been operating so well in the zone of conscious grit. Build into your conversation a demonstration of your authentic self, your adaptability, your curiosity and growth mindset.

Best wishes

Your Mentor

Having a high level of emotional intelligence will keep you in the zone of conscious grit

Emotional intelligence is often referred to as EQ. The concept emerged from research undertaken by Daniel Goleman in the 1990s. Like curiosity and adaptability that we discussed in Chapter Seven, emotional intelligence can be learned. In his book, *Emotional Intelligence*[31], Goleman describes four categories of emotional intelligence skills: self-awareness, self-management, social awareness, and relationship management.

---

31   Goleman, D 1995, *Emotional Intelligence: Why It Can Matter More Than IQ*, Bantam Books, New York

Self-Management. The ability to keep disruptive emotions in check and act thoughtfully and appropriately, congruent with your values.

Self-Awareness. Understanding your own emotions and the effects on your performance.

Social Awareness. Recognising and interpreting other people's non-verbal cues so that you can see their perspective, know how they feel and can empathise with them.

Relationship Management. Using your awareness of your own emotions and those of others to manage interactions successfully.

Your level of emotional intelligence will influence the way you manage yourself and your relationships with people. Having a high EQ will help you stay in the zone of conscious grit in a positive way. It's also a mechanism for getting you back in the zone if things go awry.

When you're in the zone of conscious grit, things may be going so well for you that you forget to put your foot on the brake. If you don't brake in time, you might hit something. You might get whiplash. The things on the seat behind you may fall off and be damaged. The person behind you on the road may run into you. Your screeching brakes will draw unwanted attention. Rather than speeding up and then slamming your foot on the brake, you can take a calm and measured approach.

You can avoid all this if you have a high level of emotional intelligence. You can also use high emotional intelligence to fix up the damage if you don't brake. You can use EQ to regulate momentum from being in the zone of conscious grit so that you don't have to slam on the brakes.

This table will help you understand the connection between conscious grit, overdone conscious grit and emotional intelligence.

Overdone Conscious Grit	Which of Goleman's Emotional Intelligence categories could help
Inability to let go when it's sensible to do so. Being **tenacious** about everything and for all situations and contexts.	Self-awareness and relationship management
Your opinion might not always be right or give the best results. You might be so **determined** to impress your perspective on others that you become angry.	Self-management and relationship management
Persisting, to invest more and more resources over an extended period of time, but there just won't be a return.	Self-management
Being **resilient** repeatedly without any reflection about why you need to bounce back so often.	Self-management and self-awareness
Planning to the ultimate degree in an intense way. Planning everything and not involving or considering others.	Self-management and relationship management
Future focus is single visioned; there is no evidence of adaptability, curiosity or growth mindset.	Self-management and relationship management

How do you measure up?

If you are displaying any of the following, it is possible that you have a low level of emotional intelligence:

- having emotional outbursts that are out of proportion to whatever is going on at the time
- having difficulty listening to others

- becoming argumentative quickly
- blaming others
- refusing to see others' points of view
- difficulty maintaining relationships.

Your level of emotional intelligence can be assessed by completing a specially designed tool. Even if your level of emotional intelligence is high, it is very likely that your scores won't be high in each of the domains. There is always something for us lifelong learners to be working on!

I recommend that you complete an EQ assessment and write down the areas that you want to work on. As noted, investing in a coach will often bring you rewards.

Daniel Goleman and Richard Boyatzis developed a 360 degree assessment tool called the Emotional Social Competency Inventory (ESCI). This tool is managed by Korn Ferry and can be accessed here: https://www.kornferry.com/about-us/consultants

Conscious grit plus high emotional intelligence. What could go wrong?

Well, we are all human.

We all mess up at some point. You need to know what to do if you mess up. You cannot just walk away and leave the mess. If you mess up, you need to fess up and fix up.

Cleaning up the mess can take many forms and you need to decide what you are going to use and make it specific for the situation.

You don't want to be the person who has a reputation for making a mess and not cleaning it up. It's bad for your reputation and your self-esteem. Conversely, cleaning up your mess reinforces your authenticity and integrity.

When I've made a mess, my go-to tool is to speak with the others involved face-to-face. I know that I'm not effective on the phone in those situations. Video communication is better than phone because at least you can see body language, but my preference is to meet face-to-face over a good coffee.

Unintentionally, I made a mess some years ago. I successfully applied for an internal role that someone else thought they would get. There was a definite 'vibe' in the office for a couple of days. I went into the other person's office and shut the door. I acknowledged her disappointment. The next day a bunch of flowers was on my desk. She appreciated that I had reached out and acknowledged her pain. The 'vibe' in the office disappeared.

Postscript to this story is that they were spring flowers and I have an allergy to them! I sneezed a lot, until we both laughed and agreed the flowers needed to go to her office! They had done their job.

Fess up and fix up using situational leadership

The concept of choosing a leadership style that will be most effective — even if it's just for the situation — is important here. The term situational leadership is relevant to us whether you are managing yourself or managing other people. It's relevant whether you are at work, at home, or in the community. You need to choose what approach you're going to use for any specific situation. If you've overdone conscious grit and have put others offside, you might consider using a different leadership style.

If you know that you've messed up, you might need to try a style of leadership that is gentler than the one you've been using. You might've messed up because you haven't included other people or have ignored advice from others. It's about shifting your style so that you can demonstrate you know there's another way to do things. The two that I'm going to share with you are servant leadership and quiet leadership.

The concept of servant leadership has been around for a long time. It is a style in which you lead by putting the needs of your team first. In 1970, Robert K Greenleaf[32] proposed ten principles of servant leadership: listening, empathy, healing, awareness, persuasion, conceptualisation, foresight, stewardship, commitment to the growth of people, and building community. Some people adopt the style of servant leadership as their main leadership style.

There are six simple ways to put servant leadership into practice when cleaning up a mess.

1. Lead by example. By tackling the mess, you signal to other people that you expect everybody can, and is allowed to, mess up. But you are also signalling that there is an expectation that each will clean up their own mess.

2. Show people why their job is important. Speak to, acknowledge and include all individuals in all roles in the team or organisation. Even when fixing up a mess and you are not happy!

---

32   Greenleaf, RK 1977, *Servant Leadership: A Journey into the Nature of Legitimate Power and Greatness*, Paulist Press, New York

3. Encourage employee engagement. Help people know that it is okay for them to bring their ideas in; their ideas might help to fix the mess.

4. Help your team grow and develop. Make sure that they have opportunities to continue to learn. Treat any mess as a catalyst moment and a learning opportunity.

5. Care for your team members at a personal level. Create psychological safety. Let them know that they can talk to you. It's easier to fix a mess when it's identified early and not hidden because someone is scared.

6. Ask for feedback. Put in some kind of system where it's common practice for feedback to be offered to you and for you to provide feedback to others. In doing this you are acknowledging that perfection isn't the aim — continually improving is.

Here is an example of servant leadership applied to a 'mess up, fess up and fix up' scenario.

Meet Bob.

Bob is a team leader. He has been under intense pressure to improve productivity. His bonus for the year is dependent on him doing so.

He is also pressured at home. His partner is desperate for him to achieve the bonus and finish the kitchen renovation.

One Friday morning, Bob, who normally sits firmly in the zone of conscious grit, calls everyone together and behaves badly. He overdoes determination and tenacity. He raises his voice and hands out a document that shows how the team needs to immediately change their work practices. Fifty per cent of the staff are having a rostered day off and Bob tells the others to let their colleagues know that things are changing.

On Monday, the work environment is flat and quiet. Most of the staff spend the morning clustered in little groups trying to figure out how to implement Bob's changes but they have little enthusiasm for doing so.

Bob has messed up. He has done well when in the zone of conscious grit, up until now. But the additional pressure coming from both work and home tipped him over the edge for a time. Fortunately, Bob has heard about Servant Leadership. This is what he does.

He calls another meeting. He apologises for his out of character behaviour and asks for input from the team about how to meet the required productivity increases.

He speaks with every member of the team including administration staff, store people, tradesmen, and team leaders. He asks them questions about how their job is going and shows that he knows their job is important. He apologises to those who were on an RDO last Friday for meeting with the other staff without them present. He asks for any improvements they could suggest for the workplace. He writes the suggestions on a whiteboard in a common area and over the next month works through them with the team.

Bob also asks what development needs they have. He hears that they are confused about the direction of the business. He organises for the CEO to come and speak with them as a group, creating an opportunity to both listen to, and ask questions of, the CEO. He sees that Emily is wounded from his 'performance' on Friday. He senses that she has withdrawn. He offers to meet with her in a place where she is comfortable to talk through her reaction. He does this in a way that shows he is genuinely sorry for upsetting her. Bob is demonstrating Servant Leadership.

I have had success combining Servant Leadership with some elements of a leadership style that David Rock[33] promotes in *Quiet Leadership*. His premise is that you can improve the performance of people by inspiring them to have input to the solution.

Rock believes that you need to acknowledge there is a mess — theirs or yours — but then focus on the solution rather than the problem. He says that focusing on the problem is only useful if you are trying to fix a piece of machinery and know what components you have to have. For example, you might need widgets to fix your tractor oil leak. Focusing on the problem will help you know which widgets you need to fix it.

Where relationships are involved, you need to focus on solutions and engage other people in discussion. People will see your humility in those discussions and recognise that you are trying to fix the mess that you've made.

Rock says that having conversations in the right way is important. He advises to take a humble approach. In the scenario above, Bob could say to Emily, 'I need to talk to you about how I behaved on Friday. I messed up. Is now a good time to have that conversation?'

When you are having conversations in quiet leadership, you listen, capture anybody's 'aha' moments, and speak in a way that is sensitive and solution focused.

---

33 Rock, D 2006, *Quiet Leadership: Six Steps to Transforming Performance at Work*, Harper Collins, New York

This is a great technique to apply at home, with the family. All the family can participate, and each member's contribution is valued and considered with respect for their intent and courage in putting their ideas forward.

I have a simple four step model for mess up, fess up and fix up.

Step 1	Define the mess	
Step 2	Dissect the mess into smaller pieces so you can see and understand	Fess up to whoever you need to – you can choose the best time to do this. It might be best at the same time as Step 1, or you might want to do it after Step 2 when you understand what you are dealing with. Or after Step 3 when you have figured out the extent of the damage and have a plan of action.
Step 3	Figure out what each piece needs to fix it or improve the situation	
Step 4	Deliver on your promise to correct the problem; don't give up until it's complete	

The easy part of this is to figure out that you've made a mess and what you're going to do about it, but the tricky part is fessing up. That involves other human beings, and you know from reading Chapter Six that your fellow humans are going to go for emotion before reason. Their amygdala is triggered. They might be in fight-mode immediately. You might also be in that mode, so you need to figure out how you are going to maintain your composure.

Have you ever been faced with a situation and had an emotional response where you thought, 'I don't know what came over me!'? Brain scientists call this an emotional hijacking – the emotional centre of your brain takes over when you didn't expect it. Have you ever laughed uncontrollably, felt like you couldn't stop and didn't know what you were laughing at? Even though that might be positive – that is, you're laughing – it's still uncontrolled and it's an emotional reaction.

Get into shape to fess up and fix up

To be unstoppable, you need to get into the zone of conscious grit and stay there. I know there are going to be tough situations that arise at work, at home and in your life generally. Developing a high level of emotional intelligence will help, along with all the other tools and tips I've given you along the way, including having a growth mindset, setting smart goals, being your authentic self, being adaptable and curious.

The good news is that emotional intelligence can be learned. So if you take an assessment and find that your score is low, there are lots of simple things you can do to develop the neural pathways related to emotional intelligence. If your score is high you can do specific things to keep those neural pathways strong.

Here are some ideas:

- Be grateful and show your gratitude to others.
- Figure out what causes stress for YOU and find ways to manage it.
- Be aware of the body language and tone of voice of others; these are all signs that will help guide your interactions and responses.
- Give back; seek to do good in exchange for nothing.
- Honestly reflect on how you did each day.
- Look for meaning in everyday events.

- Be a people watcher; that will help you know how to engage with everyone.
- Encourage feedback and criticism and value it for what it is: an opportunity to improve.
- Breathe before you speak and don't talk over others.
- Exercise to release feel-good chemicals and increase your mood.
- Use meditation and guided visualisations.
- Learn how to respectfully disagree with others.

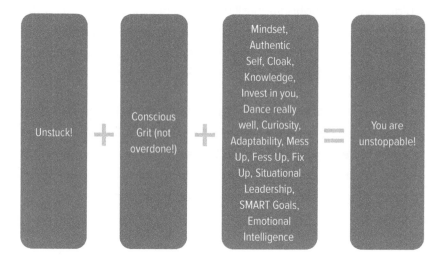

Unstoppable

Sounds pretty final doesn't it. It's certainly not final! Like being in the zones of unconscious grit and conscious grit, being unstoppable is a busy place to be. It's not a specific bus stop or train station. It's a zone.

I am not going to kid you. Being in the zone of unstoppable doesn't mean that your life is going to be perfectly awesome every day from herein. That's just not realistic. As Forrest Gump said in the movie of the same name, 'Life is like a box of chocolates. You never know what you're gonna get.' You always need to expect the unexpected. But you know now how to get into the zone of conscious grit; once there you have the tools to deal with the unexpected.

Even in the mundane grind of everyday life, you will have days when you feel that you are absolutely in the sweet spot of being unstoppable. Other days, you will feel you are just on the edge of the zone and you are feeling far from being unstoppable.

There could be one or a combination of many reasons for sliding to the edge of the zone. We all have down days for no reason we can put our finger on. We all have down days for reasons we can identify – we've fought with the kids or our partner, we've lots of bills to pay, we are unwell, we are grieving, we are overloaded with 'stuff'.

These are the times to remember that it's okay to feel that way sometimes. Just remember that you are in the unstoppable zone and your slide to the edge is only temporary. Of course, if these down days continue – go to see a professional.

At the start of this book, I gave some metaphors for being in the zone of conscious grit.

They were you:

- feel like you are swimming in treacle
- feel like you are spinning your wheels
- feel like you are carrying water in a sieve

Here are some metaphors for being in the zone of unstoppable.

You feel like:

- you want to eagerly peel off the layers of life, as you would an onion, to see what they hold; you know some layers might make you cry, but you know you have the tools to deal with it
- you can't wait to walk down a hallway with lots of closed doors – so you can open them and see what opportunities there are
- the power to write YOUR story every day is in your hands
- you are well equipped to live life like a roller coaster; you appreciate the ups AND the downs
- you have all the equipment you need to swim against the tide when you need to
- you have a delicate but detectable spring in your step.

There is a poem by Edgar Guest[34] that I think is perfect to end this chapter. Edgar Guest is sometimes thought of as the person who first brought the concept of personal development to the fore. He started writing poetry in 1904 when he was in his early 20s. This poem paints a lovely picture of what it is to feel unstoppable.

---

34   https://www.familyfriendpoems.com/poet/edgar-guest/poems/

It Couldn't Be Done

Somebody said that it couldn't be done
But he with a chuckle replied
That 'maybe it couldn't,' but he would be one
Who wouldn't say so till he'd tried.
So he buckled right in with the trace of a grin
On his face. If he worried he hid it.
He started to sing as he tackled the thing
That couldn't be done, and he did it!

Somebody scoffed: 'Oh, you'll never do that;
At least no one ever has done it;'
But he took off his coat and he took off his hat
And the first thing we knew he'd begun it.
With a lift of his chin and a bit of a grin,
Without any doubting or quiddit,
He started to sing as he tackled the thing
That couldn't be done, and he did it.

There are thousands to tell you it cannot be done,
There are thousands to prophesy failure,
There are thousands to point out to you one by one,
The dangers that wait to assail you.
But just buckle in with a bit of a grin,
Just take off your coat and go to it;
Just start in to sing as you tackle the thing

That 'cannot be done,' and you'll do it.

Epilogue

I've aimed to take you on a journey that has, at its core, a personal event in my life. It was the catalyst for me to move from stuck, to unstuck, and then to unstoppable.

We are all human, however, and if you feel vulnerable and that it's too hard to move, know that you are not alone. If ever there was a time to feel vulnerable, it is indeed when you are on the cusp of publishing your first book. And it contains your personal story and learnings. That is me, right now. I am confident, however, that the greater good will prevail and that many individuals will benefit from knowing that it is possible to go from stuck to unstuck and then to being unstoppable.

If you take nothing else from this book, take that you can indeed tip from that zone of trying hard and not getting where you need to go – to the zone of conscious grit where future focus and planning will give you the boost you need. Once you are there, your mood will lift, you will see progress, and you will soak up the additional skills and knowledge you need to be unstoppable.

In my case, when I embraced this approach that I have now coined as 'stuck to unstoppable', I gained qualifications, employment, career advancement, stable housing, confidence, leadership skills, right brain capabilities, a successful side hustle in my Celebrant business and the experience to enable me to establish my own practice, Everywhen Solutions.

George Bernard Shaw said, 'Life wasn't meant to be easy.' But life wasn't meant to be ridiculously hard either. When you read this book and do the personal projects, you're going to have strong personal insight. You will know what you need to do to be the best leader of both yourself and others. You will not have regrets about 'should have, could have'. Every step you take will be a step towards a future that you want. Remember that every response you make, to any event, crafts the outcome. Don't be despondent about the past. Although the past is gone and settled, the future is still up for grabs. You have control over your choices, decisions, and responses. You might need to find and catch a tipping point. If so, do it. That's what unstoppable means to me.

Think about this. In the last twenty-four hours, you have prioritised some things and neglected others. You've been doing this since the day you were born, and you'll continue to do this 'til the day you die. Think about your past. Everything you have focused on has improved, but everything you have neglected has either stagnated or deteriorated. If you want to live your best life, commit to being unstoppable. Then you can choose what you want to change and choose to get into the zone of conscious grit to make it happen. You are powerful. You are in the driver's seat. You choose to take the handbrake off or not.

In this book, I bring you my experience in life – both at home and in my career. I'm not a psychologist, and I know there are many reasons people get stuck. I want you to reach out to a professional if, in your process to become unstuck on the road to unstoppable, you feel that you need additional professional support. There are some challenging concepts in my book, and they have challenged me as I've discovered them over many years. It's a big step to realise that only you are responsible for you.

When you dig into your limiting beliefs, you will find pain. With that pain, though, comes a deeper understanding of why you do the things you do. You may not be able to bring yourself to involve others, but I found out it was necessary and that I could not do it alone.

I would love to hear about your journey, your successes and your challenges as you use my model of unconscious and conscious grit and work through the personal projects in each chapter. I would love to hear about your tipping point and where you found it.

I offer programs to help individuals and teams grow and develop, through individual coaching and workshops. Sometimes, individuals and teams choose to complete a diagnostic to start the process. I am an accredited consultant in DISC Advanced® and a certified trainer in i4 Neuroleader™ Model.

If you would like my support or want to contribute your thoughts, please contact me at www.everywhensolutions.com.au or gail@everywhensolutions.com.au. I would love to hear from you.

I hope that everyone who is feeling stuck finds inspiration in this book. Remember, you can't steer a parked car. Everything you need is within you. You can make it happen.

My final gift to you is this mantra:

I am. I can. I will. Watch me.

Books and articles mentioned in *Conscious Grit*

Against All Odds, Craig Challen and Richard Harris

Authentic: How to Be Yourself and Why It Matters, Stephen Joseph

Becoming, Michelle Obama

Cracking the Curiosity Code: The Key to Unlocking Human Potential, Diane Hamilton

Emotional Intelligence, Daniel Goleman

Hardwired Humans, Andrew O'Keeffe

Leadership Is Upside Down, Silvia Damiano

Maximum Confidence, Jack Canfield

Mindset, Carol Dweck

Servant Leadership: A Journey into the Nature of Legitimate Power and Greatness, Robert K Greenleaf

She Means Business, Carrie Green

The Gifts of Imperfection, Brené Brown

The Inner Game of Tennis, W Timothy Gallwey

The *Power of Vulnerability: Teachings on Authenticity, Connection and Courage:* Audio CD – Unabridged, 2 January 2013, Brené Brown

The Success Principles, Jack Canfield

'A conversation with Phil Keoghan. Adventurer. Storyteller. Host of the Amazing Race', Interview with Zoe Kors, www.marandapleasantmedia.com

'Leaving ego at the door when it comes to business', Angela Kambouris, https://leadersinheels.com/category/career/self-development/page/5/

Lifeline, www.lifeline.org.au

Acknowledgements

If you are reading the acknowledgements page you are at the end. So you know about the zone of conscious grit! And I can tell you I have needed to work hard to keep in that zone to write this book! I followed my own advice and reached out to others to help me - and I got it done. My heartfelt thanks and gratitude to the wonderful professionals who I've worked with; Kath Walters who helped me get the ideas out of my head, editors Christine Edwards and Kylie Carman-Brown for their expertise and for persevering with a new author, Sylvie Blair for so smoothly coordinating the design and publishing process and my oh- so-patient cover designer Olivia Duggan. To my BETA readers - I had no idea I was asking you to do such a major task and I thank you from the bottom of my heart for your dedication to the task, feedback and testimonials.

Lots of love and so many thanks go to my husband Tony who tolerated and supported my obsession with this project in so many ways over many months.

My final words are for two very special people who have trusted me to publicly tell part of our shared journey. To Jason and Alanna, 'thanks", "with gratitude" and 'I love you so much' is nowhere near enough. But you will both understand the words of Billy Joel - 'I intend to hold you for the longest time.'

Lightning Source UK Ltd.
Milton Keynes UK
UKHW020654080321
379980UK00015B/1874

9 780645 115703